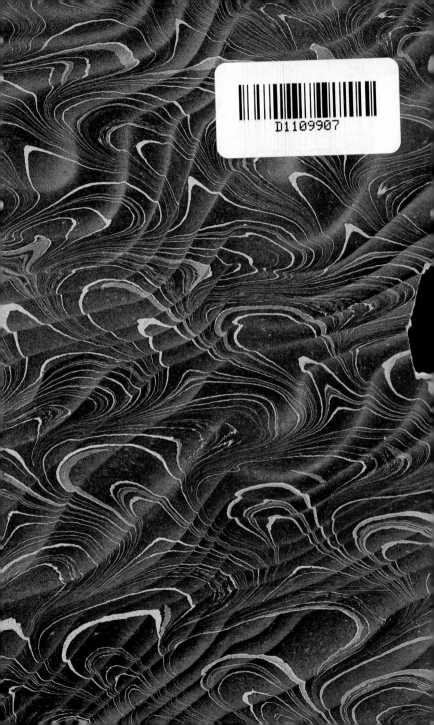

D1109907

Riverby Edition

THE WRITINGS OF
JOHN BURROUGHS

WITH PORTRAITS AND MANY ILLUSTRATIONS

VOLUME X

Walt Whitman
taken from life 1863
war time Washington
D C

to Horace L Traubel
from his friend W W
June 1888-

Mr. Whitman at the Age of 44

THE WRITINGS

OF

JOHN BURROUGHS

X

WHITMAN: A STUDY

BOSTON AND NEW YORK

HOUGHTON, MIFFLIN AND COMPANY

The Riverside Press, Cambridge

Fairleigh Dickinson
University Library

MADISON, NEW JERSEY

PS 1220
F 04
Library
Director's
Office

28660
v/o

Copyright 1896 *and* 1904

By John Burroughs

All rights reserved

CONTENTS

"*All original art is self-regulated, and no original art can be regulated from without ; it carries its own counterpoise, and does not receive it from elsewhere.*" — TAINE.

"*If you want to tell good Gothic, see if it has the sort of roughness and largeness and nonchalance, mixed in places with the exquisite tenderness which seems always to be the sign manual of the broad vision and massy power of men who can see past the work they are doing, and betray here and there something like disdain for it.*" — RUSKIN.

"*Formerly, during the period termed classic, when literature was governed by recognized rules, he was considered the best poet who had composed the most perfect work, the most beautiful poem, the most intelligible, the most agreeable to read, the most complete in every respect, — the Æneid, the Gerusalemme, a fine tragedy. To-day something else is wanted. For us the greatest poet is he who in his works most stimulates the reader's imagination and reflection, who excites him the most himself to poetize. The greatest poet is not he who has done the best, it is he who suggests the most ; he, not all of whose meaning is at first obvious, and who leaves you much to desire, to explain, to study, much to complete in your turn.*" — SAINTE-BEUVE.

LIST OF ILLUSTRATIONS

WHITMAN

WHITMAN

PRELIMINARY

I

THE writing of this preliminary chapter, and the final survey and revision of my Whitman essay, I am making at a rustic house I have built at a wild place a mile or more from my home upon the river. I call this place Whitman Land, because in many ways it is typical of my poet, — an amphitheatre of precipitous rock, slightly veiled with a delicate growth of verdure, inclosing a few acres of prairie-like land, once the site of an ancient lake, now a garden of unknown depth and fertility. Elemental ruggedness, savageness, and grandeur, combined with wonderful tenderness, modernness, and geniality. There rise the gray scarred cliffs, crowned here and there with a dead hemlock or pine, where, morning after morning, I have seen the bald eagle perch, and here at their feet this level area of tender humus, with three perennial springs of delicious cold water flowing in its margin ; a huge granite bowl filled with the elements and potencies of life. The scene has a strange fascination for me, and holds me here day after day. From the highest point of rocks I can overlook a long stretch of the river and of the farming country beyond; I can hear owls hoot, hawks scream, and roosters crow. Birds of the garden and orchard meet birds of the forest upon the shaggy cedar posts that uphold my porch. At dusk the call of the whip-poor-will mingles with the chorus of the pickerel frogs, and in the morning I hear through the robins' cheerful burst the somber plaint of the mourning-dove. When I tire of my manuscript, I walk in the woods, or climb the rocks, or help the men clear up the ground, piling and burning the stumps and rubbish. This scene and situation, so primitive and secluded, yet so touched with and adapted to civilization, responding to the moods of both sides of the life and imagination of a modern man, seems, I repeat, typical in many ways of my poet, and is a veritable Whitman land. Whitman does not to me suggest the wild and unkempt as he seems to do to many; he suggests the cosmic and the elemental, and this is one of the dominant thoughts that run through my dissertation. Scenes of power and savagery in nature were more welcome to him, probably more stimulating to him, than the scenes of the pretty and placid, and he cherished the hope that he had put into his "Leaves" some of the tonic and fortifying quality of Nature in her more grand and primitive aspects.

His wildness is only the wildness of the great

primary forces from which we draw our health and strength. Underneath all his unloosedness, or free launching forth of himself, is the sanity and repose of nature.

II

I first became acquainted with Whitman's poetry through the columns of the old "Saturday Press" when I was twenty or twenty-one years old (1858 or 1859). The first things I remember to have read were "There was a child went forth," "This Compost," "As I ebb'd with the Ocean of Life," "Old Ireland," and maybe a few others. I was attracted by the new poet's work from the first. It seemed to let me into a larger, freer air than I found in the current poetry. Meeting Bayard Taylor about this time, I spoke to him about Whitman. "Yes," he said, "there is something in him, but he is a man of colossal egotism."

A few years later a friend sent me a copy of the Thayer & Eldridge edition of "Leaves of Grass" of 1860. It proved a fascinating but puzzling book to me. I grazed upon it like a colt upon a mountain, taking what tasted good to me, and avoiding what displeased me, but having little or no conception of the purport of the work as a whole. I found passages and whole poems here and there that I never tired of reading, and that gave a strange fillip to my moral and intellectual nature, but nearly as many passages and poems puzzled or repelled me.

WHITMAN

My absorption of Emerson had prepared me in a measure for Whitman's philosophy of life, but not for the ideals of character and conduct which he held up to me, nor for the standards in art to which the poet perpetually appealed. Whitman was Emerson translated from the abstract into the concrete. There was no privacy with Whitman; he never sat me down in a corner with a cozy, comfortable shut-in feeling, but he set me upon a hill or started me upon an endless journey. Wordsworth had been my poet of nature, of the sequestered and the idyllic; but I saw that here was a poet of a larger, more fundamental nature, indeed of the Cosmos itself. Not a poet of dells and fells, but of the earth and the orbs. This much soon appeared to me, but I was troubled by the poet's apparent "colossal egotism," by his attitude toward evil, declaring himself "to be the poet of wickedness also;" by his seeming attraction toward the turbulent and the disorderly; and, at times, by what the critics had called his cataloguing style of treatment.

When I came to meet the poet himself, which was in the fall of 1863, I felt less concern about these features of his work; he was so sound and sweet and gentle and attractive as a man, and withal so wise and tolerant, that I soon came to feel the same confidence in the book that I at once placed in its author, even in the parts which I did not understand. I saw that the work and the man

6

were one, and that the former must be good as the latter was good. There was something in the manner in which both the book and its author carried themselves under the sun, and in the way they confronted America and the present time, that convinced beyond the power of logic or criticism.

The more I saw of Whitman, and the more I studied his " Leaves," the more significance I found in both, and the clearer it became to me that a new type of a man and a new departure in poetic literature were here foreshadowed. There was something forbidding, but there was something vital and grand back of it. I found to be true what the poet said of himself, —

"Bearded, sunburnt, gray-neck'd, forbidding, I have
        arrived,
To be wrestled with as I pass for the solid prizes of the
        universe,
For such I afford whoever can persevere to win them."

I have persevered in my study of the poet, though balked many times, and the effect upon my own mental and spiritual nature has been great; no such "solid prizes" in the way of a broader outlook upon life and nature, and, I may say, upon art, has any poet of my time afforded me. There are passages or whole poems in the "Leaves" which I do not yet understand ("Sleep-Chasings" is one of them), though the language is as clear as daylight; they are simply too subtle or elusive for me; but my confidence in the logical soundness of the book is so complete that I do not trouble myself at all about these things.

III

I would fain make these introductory remarks to my essay a sort of window through which the reader may get a fairly good view of what lies beyond. If he does not here get any glimpse or suggestion of what pleases him, or of what he is looking for, it will hardly be worth while for him to trouble himself further.

A great many readers, perhaps three fourths of the readers of current poetry, and not a few of the writers thereof, cannot stand Whitman at all, or see any reason for his being. To such my essay, if it ever comes to their notice, will be a curiosity, maybe an offense. But I trust it will meet with a different reception at the hands of the smaller but rapidly growing circle of those who are beginning to turn to Whitman as the most imposing and significant figure in our literary annals.

The rapidly growing Whitman literature attests the increasing interest to which I refer. Indeed, it seems likely that by the end of the century the literature which will have grown up around the name of this man will surpass in bulk and value that which has grown up around the name of any other man of letters born within the century.

PRELIMINARY

When Mr. Stedman wrote his essay upon the poet early in the eighties, he referred to the mass of this literature. It has probably more than doubled in volume in the intervening years : since Whitman's death in the spring of '92, it has been added to by William Clark's book upon the poet, Professor Trigg's study of Browning and Whitman, and the work of that accomplished critic and scholar, so lately gone to his rest, John Addington Symonds. This last is undoubtedly the most notable contribution that has yet been made, or is likely very soon to be made, to the Whitman literature. Mr. Symonds declares that "Leaves of Grass," which he first read at the age of twenty-five, influenced him more than any other book has done, except the Bible, — more than Plato, more than Goethe.

When we remember that the man who made this statement was eminently a man of books, deeply read in all literatures, his testimony may well offset that of a score of our home critics who find nothing worthy or helpful in Whitman's work. One positive witness in such a matter outweighs any number of negative ones.

IV

For making another addition to the growing Whitman literature, I have no apology to offer. I know well enough that "writing and talk" cannot

9

"prove" a poet; that he must be his own proof or
be forgotten; and my main purpose in writing about
Whitman, as in writing about nature, is to tell readers what I have found there, with the hope of in-
ducing them to look for themselves. At the same
time, I may say that I think no modern poet so
much needs to be surrounded by an atmosphere of
comment and interpretation, through which readers
may approach him, as does Whitman. His work
sprang from a habit or attitude of mind quite foreign
to that with which current literature makes us familiar, — so germinal is it, and so little is it beholden
to the formal art we so assiduously cultivate. The
poet says his work "connects lovingly with prece-
dents," but it does not connect lovingly with any
body of poetry of this century. "Leaves of Grass"
is bound to be a shock to the timid and pampered
taste of the majority of current readers. I would
fain lessen this shock by interposing my own pages
of comment between the book and the public. The
critic can say so many things the poet cannot. He
can explain and qualify and analyze, whereas the
creative artist can only hint or project. The poet
must hasten on, he must infold and bind together,
he must be direct and synthetic in every act. Reflection and qualification are not for him, but action,
emotion, volition, the procreant blending and sur-
render. He works as Nature does, and gives us
reality in every line.

PRELIMINARY

Whitman says: —

"I charge you forever reject those who would expound
    me, for I cannot expound myself."

The type of mind of Whitman's, which seldom or
never emerges as a mere mentality, an independent
thinking and knowing faculty, but always as a personality, always as a complete human entity, never
can expound itself, because its operations are synthetic and not analytic, its mainspring is love and
not mere knowledge. In his prose essay called "A
Backward Glance o'er Travel'd Roads," appended
to the final edition of his poems, Whitman has not
so much sought to expound himself as to put his
reader in possession of his point of view, and of
the considerations that lie back of his work, This
chapter might render much that I have written
superfluous, were there not always a distinct gain
in seeing an author through another medium, or in
getting the equivalents of him in the thoughts and
ideals of a kindred and sympathetic mind. But I
have not consciously sought to expound Whitman,
any more than in my other books I have sought to
expound the birds or wild nature. I have written
out some things that he means to me, and the pleasure and profit I have found in his pages.

There is no end to what can be drawn out of him.
It has been said and repeated that he was not a
thinker, and yet I find more food for thought in

him than in all other poets. It has been often said and repeated that he is not a poet, and yet the readers that respond to him the most fully appear to be those in whom the poetic temperament is paramount. I believe he supplies in fuller measure that pristine element, something akin to the unbreathed air of mountain and shore, which makes the arterial blood of poetry and literature, than any other modern writer.

V

We can make little of Whitman unless we allow him to be a law unto himself, and seek him through the clews which he himself brings. When we try him by current modes, current taste, and demand of him formal beauty, formal art, we are disappointed. But when we try him by what we may call the scientific standard, the standard of organic nature, and demand of him the vital and the characteristic, — demand of him that he have a law of his own, and fulfill that law in the poetic sphere, — the result is quite different.

More than any other poet, Whitman is what we make him; more than any other poet, his greatest value is in what he suggests and implies, rather than in what he portrays; and more than any other poet must he wait to be understood by the growth of the taste of himself. "I make the only growth by which I can be appreciated," he truly says.

His words are like the manna that descended

upon the Israelites, "in which were all manner of tastes ; and every one found in it what his palate was chiefly pleased with. If he desired fat in it, he had it. In it the young men tasted bread; the old men honey ; and the children oil." Many young men, — poets, artists, teachers, preachers, — have testified that they have found bread in Whitman, the veritable bread of life ; others have found honey, sweet poetic morsels ; and not a few report having found only gall.

VI

In considering an original work like "Leaves of Grass," the search is always for the grounds upon which it is to be justified and explained. These grounds in this work are not easy to find; they lie deeper than the grounds upon which the popular poets rest. Because they are not at once seen, many readers have denied that there are any such grounds. But to deny a basis of reality to a work with the history of "Leaves of Grass," and a basis well grounded on æsthetic and artistic principles, is not to be thought of.

The more the poet eludes us, the more we know he has his hiding-place somewhere. The more he denies our standards, the more we know he has standards of his own which we must discover; the more he flouts at our literary conventions, the more we must press him for his own principles and

13

methods. How does he justify himself to himself? Could any sane man have written the Children of Adam poems who was not sustained by deepest moral and æsthetic convictions? It is the business of the critic to search for these principles and convictions, and not shirk the task by ridicule and denial.

VII

If there was never any change in taste, if it always ran in the same channels, — indeed, if it did not at times run in precisely opposite channels, — there would be little hope that Walt Whitman's poetry would ever find any considerable number of readers. But one of the laws that dominate the progress of literature, as Edmond Schérer says, is incessant change, not only in thought and ideas, but in taste and the starting-points of art. A radical and almost violent change in these respects is indicated by Whitman, — a change which is in unison with many things in modern life and morals, but which fairly crosses the prevailing taste in poetry and in art. No such dose of realism and individualism under the guise of poetry has been administered to the reading public in this century. No such break with literary traditions — no such audacious attempt to tally, in a printed page, the living concrete man, an actual human presence, instead of the conscious, made-up poet — is to be found in modern literary records.

VIII

The much that I have said in the following pages about Whitman's radical differences from other poets — his changed attitude toward the universe, his unwonted methods and aims — might seem to place him upon a ground so unique and individual as to contradict my claims for his breadth and universality. The great poets stand upon common ground; they excel along familiar lines, they touch us, and touch us deeply, at many points. What always saves Whitman is his enormous endowment of what is "commonest, nearest, easiest," — his atmosphere of the common day, the common life, and his fund of human sympathy and love. He is strange because he gives us the familiar in such a direct, unexpected manner. His "Leaves" are like some new fruit that we have never before tasted. It is the product of another clime, another hemisphere. The same old rains and dews, the same old sun and soil, nursed it, yet in so many ways how novel and strange! We certainly have to serve a certain apprenticeship to this poet, familiarize ourselves with his point of view and with his democratic spirit, before we can make much of him. The spirit in which we come to him from the other poets — the poets of art and culture — is for the most part unfriendly to him. There is something rude, strange, and unpoetic about him at first sight that is sure to give most

readers of poetry a shock. I think one might come
to him from the Greek poets, or the old Hebrew
or Oriental bards, with less shock than from our
modern delicate and refined singers; because the old
poets were more simple and elemental, and aimed
less at the distilled dainties of poetry, than the modern. They were full of action, too, and volition,
— of that which begets and sustains life. Whitman's poetry is almost entirely the expression of
will and personality, and runs very little to intellectual subtleties and refinements. It fulfills itself
in our wills and characters, rather than in our taste.

IX

Whitman will always be a strange and unwonted
figure among his country's poets, and among English poets generally, — a cropping out again, after so
many centuries, of the old bardic prophetic strain.
Had he dropped upon us from some other sphere,
he could hardly have been a greater surprise and
puzzle to the average reader or critic. Into a literature that was timid, imitative, conventional, he
fell like leviathan into a duck-pond, and the com-
motion and consternation he created there have not
yet subsided. All the reigning poets in this country except Emerson denied him, and many of our
minor poets still keep up a hostile sissing and cack-
ling. He will probably always be more or less a
stumbling-block to the minor poet, because of his

16

indifference to the things which to the minor poet
are all in all. He was a poet without what is called
artistic form, and without technique, as that word is
commonly understood. His method was analogous
to the dynamic method of organic nature, rather
than to the mechanical or constructive method of
the popular poets.

x

Of course the first thing that strikes the reader
in "Leaves of Grass" is its seeming oddity and
strangeness. If a man were to come into a dress
reception in shirt-sleeves and with his hat on, the
feature would strike us at once, and would be magnified in our eyes; we should quite forget that he
was a man, and in essentials differed but little from
the rest of us, after all. The exterior habiliments
on such occasions count for nearly everything; and
in the popular poetry rhyme, measure, and the language and manners of the poets are much more
than anything else. If Whitman did not do anything so outré as to come into a dress reception
with his coat off and his hat on, he did come into the
circle of the poets without the usual poetic habiliments. He was not dressed up at all, and he was
not at all abashed or apologetic. His air was confident and self-satisfied, if it did not at times suggest
the insolent and aggressive. It was the dress circle
that was on trial, and not Walt Whitman.

17

We could forgive a man in real life for such an audacious proceeding only on the ground of his being something extraordinary as a person, with an extraordinary message to convey; and we can pardon the poet only on precisely like grounds. He must make us forget his unwonted garb by his unique and lovable personality, and the power and wisdom of his utterance. If he cannot do this, we shall soon tire of him.

That Whitman was a personality the like of which the world has not often seen, and that his message to his country and to his race was of prime importance, are conclusions at which more and more thinking persons are surely arriving.

His want of art, of which we have heard so much, is, it seems to me, just this want of the usual trappings and dress uniform of the poets. In the essentials of art, the creative imagination, the plastic and quickening spirit, the power of identification with the thing contemplated, and the absolute use of words, he has few rivals.

XI

I make no claim that my essay is a dispassionate, disinterested view of Whitman. It will doubtless appear to many as a one-sided view, or as colored by my love for the man himself. And I shall not be disturbed if such turns out to be the case. A dispassionate view of a man like Whitman is prob-

ably out of the question in our time, or in any near
time. His appeal is so personal and direct that
readers are apt to be either violently for him or
violently against, and it will require the perspective
of more than one generation to bring out his true
significance. Still, for any partiality for its subject
which my book may show, let me take shelter behind a dictum of Goethe.

"I am more and more convinced," says the great
critic, "that whenever one has to vent an opinion
on the actions or on the writings of others, unless
this be done from a certain one-sided enthusiasm, or
from a loving interest in the person and the work,
the result is hardly worth gathering up. Sympathy and enjoyment in what we see is in fact the only
reality, and, from such reality, reality as a natural
product follows. All else is vanity."

To a loving interest in Whitman and his work,
which may indeed amount to one-sided enthusiasm, I plead guilty. This at least is real with me,
and not affected ; and, if the reality which Goethe
predicts in such cases only follows, I shall be more
than content.

XII

In the world of literature, as in the world of
physical forces, things adjust themselves after a
while, and no impetus can be given to any man's
name or fame that will finally carry it beyond the

limit of his real worth. However "one-sided" my enthusiasm for Whitman may be, or that of any of his friends may be, there is no danger but that in time he will find exactly his proper place and level. My opinion, or any man's opinion, of the works of another, is like a wind that blows for a moment across the water, heaping it up a little on the shore or else beating it down, but not in any way permanently affecting its proper level.

The adverse winds that have blown over Whitman's work have been many and persistent, and yet the tide has surely risen, his fame has slowly increased.

It will soon be forty years since he issued the first thin quarto edition of "Leaves of Grass," and, though the opposition to him has been the most fierce and determined ever recorded in our literary history, often degenerating into persecution and willful misrepresentation, yet his fame has steadily grown both at home and abroad. The impression he early made upon such men as Emerson, Thoreau, William O'Connor, Mr. Stedman, Colonel Ingersoll, and others in this country, and upon Professors Dowden and Clifford, upon Symonds, Ruskin, Tennyson, Rossetti, Lord Lytton, Mrs. Gilchrist, George Eliot, in England, has been followed by an equally deep or deeper impression upon many of the younger and bolder spirits of both hemispheres. In fact, Whitman saw his battle essentially won in his own lifetime, though his complete triumph is of course a matter of the distant future.

XIII

But let me give without further delay a fuller hint of the attitude these pages assume and hold toward the subject they discuss.

There are always, or nearly always, a few men born to each generation who embody the best thought and culture of that generation, and express it in approved literary forms. From Petrarch down to Lowell, the lives and works of these men fill the literary annals; they uphold the literary and scholarly traditions; they are the true men of letters; they are justly honored and beloved in their day and land. We in this country have recently, in the death of Dr. Holmes, mourned the loss of the last of the New England band of such men. We are all indebted to them for solace, and for moral and intellectual stimulus.

Then, much more rarely, there are born to a race or people men who are like an irruption of life from another world, who belong to another order, who bring other standards, and sow the seed of new and larger types; who are not the organs of the culture or modes of their time, and whom their times for the most part decry and disown, — the primal, original, elemental men. It is here, in my opinion, that we must place Whitman; not among the

21

minstrels and edifiers of his age, but among its prophets and saviours. He is nearer the sources of things than the popular poets, — nearer the founders and discoverers, closer akin to the large, fervent, prophetic, patriarchal men who figure in the early heroic ages. His work ranks with the great primitive books. He is of the type of the skald, the bard, the seer, the prophet. The specialization and differentiation of our latter ages of science and culture are less marked in him than in other poets. Poetry, philosophy, religion, are all inseparably blended in his pages. He is in many ways a reversion to an earlier type. Dr. Brinton has remarked that his attitude toward the principle of sex and his use of sexual imagery in his poems are the same as in the more primitive religions. Whitman was not a poet by elaboration, but by suggestion ; not an artist by formal presentation, but by spirit and conception; not a philosopher by system and afterthought, but by vision and temper.

In his " Leaves," we again hear the note of destiny, — again see the universal laws and forces exemplified in the human personality, and turned upon life with love and triumph.

XIV

The world always has trouble with its primary men, or with the men who have any primary gifts, like Emerson, Wordsworth, Browning, Tolstoi, Ib-

sen. The idols of an age are nearly always secondary men : they break no new ground; they make
no extraordinary demands; our tastes and wants are
already adjusted to their type; we understand and
approve of them at once. The primary men dis-
turb us; they are a summons and a challenge; they
break up the old order; they open up new territory
which we are to subdue and occupy; the next age
and the next make more of them. In my opinion,
the next age and the next will make more of Whitman, and the next still more, because he is in the
great world-current, in the line of the evolutionary
movement of our time. Is it at all probable that
Tennyson can ever be to any other age what he has
been to this ? Tennyson marks an expiring age, the
sunset of the feudal world. He did not share the
spirit to which the future belongs. There was not
one drop of democratic blood in his veins. To him,
the people were an hundred-headed beast.

XV

If my essay seems like one continual strain to
attain the unattainable, to compass and define Whitman, who will not be compassed and defined, I can
only say that I regret it, but could not well help it.
Talking about Whitman, Symonds said, was like
talking about the universe, and it is so. There is
somewhat incommensurable in his works. One may
not hope to speak the final word about him, to sum

him up in a sentence. He is so palpable, so real,
so near at hand, that the critic or expounder of him
promises himself an easy victory ; but before one
can close with him he is gone. He is, after all, as
subtle and baffling as the air or light.

> . . . " I will certainly elude you,
> Even while you should think you had unquestionably
>   caught me, behold !
> Already you see I have escaped from you."

It is probably this characteristic which makes
Whitman an irrepressible figure in literature ; he
will not down for friend or foe. He escapes from
all classification, and is larger than any definition
of him that has yet been given. How many times
has he been exploded by British and American critics; how many times has he been labeled and put
upon the shelf, only to reappear again as vigorous
and untranslatable as ever!

XVI

So far as Whitman stands merely for the spirit
of revolt, or of reaction against current modes in
life and literature, I have little interest in him.
As the " apostle of the rough, the uncouth," to use
Mr. Howells's words, the world would long ago
have tired of him. The irruption into letters of
the wild and lawless, or of the strained and eccen-
tric, can amuse and interest us only for a moment.

PRELIMINARY

It is because these are only momentary phases of him, as it were, and because underneath all he embraces the whole of life and ministers to it, that his fame and influence are still growing in the world. One hesitates even to call Whitman the poet of "democracy," or of "personality," or of "the modern," because such terms only half define him. He quickly escapes into that large and universal air which all great art breathes. We cannot sum him up in a phrase. He flows out on all sides, and his sympathies embrace all types and conditions of men. He is a great democrat, but, first and last and over all, he is a great man, a great nature, and deep world-currents course through him. He is distinctively an American poet, but his Americanism is only the door through which he enters upon the universal.

XVII

Call his work poetry or prose, or what you will: that it is an inspired utterance of some sort, any competent person ought to be able to see. And what else do we finally demand of any work than that it be inspired? How all questions of form and art, and all other questions, sink into insignificance beside that! The exaltation of mind and spirit shown in the main body of Whitman's work, the genuine, prophetic fervor, the intensification and amplification of the simple ego, and the resultant raising of all human values, seem to me as plain as daylight.

Whitman is to be classed among the great names by the breadth and all-inclusiveness of his theme and by his irrepressible personality. I think it highly probable that future scholars and critics will find his work fully as significant and era-marking as that of any of the few supreme names of the past. It is the culmination of an age of individualism, and, as opposites meet, it is also the best lesson in nationalism and universal charity that this century has seen.

BIOGRAPHICAL AND PERSONAL

I

WALT WHITMAN was born at West Hills, Long Island, May 30, 1819, and died at Camden, N. J., March 26, 1892. Though born in the country, most of his life was passed in cities; first in Brooklyn and New York, then in New Orleans, then in Washington, and lastly in Camden, where his body is buried. It was a poet's life from first to last, — free, unhampered, unworldly, unconventional, picturesque, simple, untouched by the craze of money-getting, unselfish, devoted to others, and was, on the whole, joyfully and contentedly lived. It was a pleased and interested saunter through the world, — no hurry, no fever, no strife; hence no bitterness, no depletion, no wasted energies. A farm boy, then a school-teacher, then a printer, editor, writer, traveler, mechanic, nurse in the army hospitals, and lastly government clerk; large and picturesque of figure, slow of movement; tolerant, passive, receptive, and democratic, — of the people; in all his tastes and attractions, always aiming to walk abreast with the great laws and forces, and to live thoroughly in the free, nonchalant

spirit of his own day and land. His strain was min-
gled Dutch and English, with a decided Quaker
tinge, which came from his mother's side, and which
had a marked influence upon his work.

The spirit that led him to devote his time and
substance to the sick and wounded soldiers during
the war may be seen in that earlier incident in his
life when he drove a Broadway stage all one winter, that a disabled driver might lie by without
starving his family. It is from this episode that
the tradition of his having been a New York stage-
driver comes. He seems always to have had a special liking for this class of workmen. One of the
house surgeons of the old New York Hospital relates
that in the latter part of the fifties Whitman was
a frequent visitor at that institution, looking after
and ministering to disabled stage-drivers. "These
drivers," says the doctor, "like those of the omnibuses in London, were a set of men by themselves.
A good deal of strength, intelligence, and skillful
management of horses was required of a Broadway
stage-driver. He seems to have been decidedly a
higher order of man than the driver of the present
horse-cars. He usually had his primary education
in the country, and graduated as a thorough expert
in managing a very difficult machine, in an exceptionally busy thoroughfare.

"It was this kind of a man that so attracted Walt
Whitman that he was constantly to be seen perched

28

on the box alongside one of them going up and down Broadway. I often watched the poet and driver, as probably did many another New Yorker in those days.

"I do not wonder as much now as I did in 1860 that a man like Walt Whitman became interested in these drivers. He was not interested in the news of every-day life, — the murders and accidents and political convulsions, — but he was interested in strong types of human character. We young men had not had experience enough to understand this kind of a man. It seems to me now that we looked at Whitman simply as a kind of crank, if the word had then been invented. His talk to us was chiefly of books, and the men who wrote them: especially of poetry, and what he considered poetry. He never said much of the class whom he visited in our wards, after he had satisfied himself of the nature of the injury and of the prospect of recovery.

"Whitman appeared to be about forty years of age at that time. He was always dressed in a blue flannel coat and vest, with gray and baggy trousers. He wore a woolen shirt, with a Byronic collar, low in the neck, without a cravat, as I remember, and a large felt hat. His hair was iron gray, and he had a full beard and mustache of the same color. His face and neck were bronzed by exposure to the sun and air. He was large, and gave the impression of being a vigorous man. He was scru-

pulously careful of his simple attire, and his hands
were soft and hairy."

During the early inception of "Leaves of Grass"
he was a carpenter in Brooklyn, building and sell-
ing small frame-houses to working people. He
frequently knocked off work to write his poems.
In his life Whitman was never one of the restless,
striving sort. In this respect he was not typical
of his countrymen. All his urgency and strenuousness he reserved for his book. He seems always to have been a sort of visitor in life, noting,
observing, absorbing, keeping aloof from all ties
that would hold him, and making the most of the
hour and the place in which he happened to be.
He was in no sense a typical literary man. During
his life in New York and Brooklyn, we see him
moving entirely outside the fashionable circles, the
learned circles, the literary circles, the money-getting circles. He belongs to no set or club. He is
seen more with the laboring classes, — drivers, boatmen, mechanics, printers, — and I suspect may often
be found with publicans and sinners. He is fond
of the ferries and of the omnibuses. He is a fre-
quenter of the theatre and of the Italian opera.
Alboni makes a deep and lasting impression upon
him. It is probably to her that he writes these
lines: —

" Here take this gift,
    I was reserving it for some hero, speaker, general,

One who should serve the good old cause, the great idea,
    the progress and freedom of the race,
Some brave confronter of despots, some daring rebel;
But I see that what I was reserving belongs to you just as
    much as to any."

Elsewhere he refers to Alboni by name and speaks of her as

"The lustrous orb, Venus contralto, the blooming mother,
Sister of loftiest gods."

Some of his poems were written at the opera. The great singers evidently gave him clews and suggestions that were applicable to his own art.

His study was out of doors. He wrote on the street, on the ferry, at the seaside, in the fields, at the opera, — always from living impulses arising at the moment, and always with his eye upon the fact. He says he has read his "Leaves" to himself in the open air, and tried them by the realities of life and nature about him. Were they as real and alive as they? — this was the only question with him.

At home in his father's family in Brooklyn we see him gentle, patient, conciliatory, much looked up to by all. Neighbors seek his advice. He is cool, deliberate, impartial. A marked trait is his indifference to money matters; his people are often troubled because he lets opportunities to make money pass by. When his "Leaves" appear, his family are puzzled, do not know what to make of it. His mother thinks that, if "Hiawatha" is poetry, maybe Walt's book is, too. He never counsels with any one, and is utterly indifferent as to what people may say or think. He is not a stirring and punctual man, is always a little late; not an early riser, not prompt at dinner; always has ample time, and will not be hurried; the business gods do not receive his homage. He is gray at thirty, and is said to have had a look of age in youth, as he had a look of youth in age. He has few books, cares little for sport, never uses a gun; has no bad habits; has no entanglements with women, and apparently never contemplates marriage. It is said that during his earliest years of manhood he kept quite aloof from the "girls."

At the age of nineteen he edited "The Long Islander," published at Huntington. A recent visitor to these early haunts of Whitman gathered some reminiscences of him at this date: —

"Amid the deep revery of nature, on that mild October afternoon, we returned to the village of Huntington, there to meet the few, the very few, survivors who recall Walt's first appearance in the literary world as the editor of 'The Long Islander,' nigh sixty years ago (1838). Two of these forefathers of the hamlet clearly remembered his powerful personality, brimful of life, reveling in strength, careless of time and the world, of money and of toil;

a lover of books and of jokes; delighting to gather round him the youth of the village in his printing-room of evenings, and tell them stories and read them poetry, his own and others'. That of his own he called his 'Yawps,' a word which he after-wards made famous. Both remembered him as a delightful companion, generous to a fault, glorying in youth, negligent of his affairs, issuing 'The Long Islander' at random intervals, — once a week, once in two weeks, once in three, — until its finan-cial backers lost faith and hope and turned him out, and with him the whole office corps; for Walt himself was editor, publisher, compositor, pressman, and printer's devil, all in one."

II

Few men were so deeply impressed by our Civil War as was Whitman. It aroused all his patriotism, all his sympathies, and, as a poet, tested his power to deal with great contemporary events and scenes. He was first drawn to the seat of war on behalf of his brother, Lieutenant-Colonel George W. Whit-man, 51st New York Volunteers, who was wounded by the fragment of a shell at Fredericksburg. This was in the fall of 1862. This brought him in con-tact with the sick and wounded soldiers, and hence-forth, as long as the war lasted and longer, he devoted his time and substance to ministering to them. The first two or three years of his life in

Washington he supported himself by correspond-
ence with Northern newspapers, mainly with the
"New York Times." These letters, as well as the
weekly letters to his mother during the same period,
form an intensely pathetic and interesting record.

They contain such revelations of himself, and
such pictures of the scenes he moved among, that I
shall here quote freely from them. The following extract is from a letter written from Fredericksburg
the third or fourth day after the battle of December,
1862: —

"Spent a good part of the day in a large brick
mansion on the banks of the Rappahannock, immediately opposite Fredericksburg. It is used as
a hospital since the battle, and seems to have received only the worst cases. Out of doors, at the
foot of a tree, within ten yards of the front of the
house, I notice a heap of amputated feet, legs,
arms, hands, etc., about a load for a one-horse cart.
Several dead bodies lie near, each covered with its
brown woolen blanket. In the door-yard, toward
the river, are fresh graves, mostly of officers, their
names on pieces of barrel-staves, or broken board,
stuck in the dirt. (Most of these bodies were subsequently taken up and transported North to their
friends.)

"The house is quite crowded, everything im-
promptu, no system, all bad enough, but I have no
doubt the best that can be done; all the wounds

34

pretty bad, some frightful, the men in their old clothes, unclean and bloody. Some of the wounded are rebel officers, prisoners. One, a Mississippian, — a captain, — hit badly in leg, I talked with some time; he asked me for papers, which I gave him. (I saw him three months afterward in Washington, with leg amputated, doing well.)

"I went through the rooms, down stairs and up. Some of the men were dying. I had nothing to give at that visit, but wrote a few letters to folks home, mothers, etc. Also talked to three or four who seemed most susceptible to it, and needing it."

"December 22 to 31. — Am among the regimental, brigade, and division hospitals somewhat. Few at home realize that these are merely tents, and sometimes very poor ones, the wounded lying on the ground, lucky if their blanket is spread on a layer of pine or hemlock twigs, or some leaves. No cots; seldom even a mattress on the ground. It is pretty cold. I go around from one case to another. I do not see that I can do any good, but I cannot leave them. Once in a while some youngster holds on to me convulsively, and I do what I can for him; at any rate, stop with him and sit near him for hours, if he wishes it.

"Besides the hospitals, I also go occasionally on long tours through the camps, talking with the men, etc.; sometimes at night among the groups around the fires, in their shebang enclosures of bushes. I soon get acquainted anywhere in camp, with officers or men, and am always well used. Sometimes I go down on picket with the regiments I know best."

After continuing in front through the winter, he returns to Washington, where the wounded and sick have mainly been concentrated. The Capital city, truly, is now one huge hospital; and there Whitman establishes himself, and thenceforward, for several years, has but one daily and nightly avocation.

He alludes to writing letters by the bedside, and says: —

"I do a good deal of this, of course, writing all kinds, including love-letters. Many sick and wounded soldiers have not written home to parents, brothers, sisters, and even wives, for one reason or another, for a long, long time. Some are poor writers, some cannot get paper and envelopes; many have an aversion to writing, because they dread to worry the folks at home, — the facts about them are so sad to tell. I always encourage the men to write, and promptly write for them."

A glimpse of the scenes after Chancellorsville: —

"As I write this, in May, 1863, the wounded have begun to arrive from Hooker's command from bloody Chancellorsville. I was down among the first arrivals. The men in charge of them told me the bad cases were yet to come. If that is so, I pity them, for these are bad enough. You ought to see the scene of the wounded arriving at the landing here foot of Sixth Street at night. Two boat-loads came about half past seven last night. A little after eight, it rained a long and violent shower. The poor, pale, helpless soldiers had been debarked, and lay around on the wharf and neighborhood anywhere. The rain was, probably, grateful to them; at any rate they were exposed to it.

"The few torches light up the spectacle. All around on the wharf, on the ground, out on side places, etc., the men are lying on blankets and old quilts, with the bloody rags bound round heads, arms, legs, etc. The attendants are few, and at night few outsiders also, — only a few hard-worked transportation men and drivers. (The wounded are getting to be common, and people grow callous.) The men, whatever their condition, lie there, and patiently wait till their turn comes to be taken up. Near by the ambulances are now arriving in clusters, and one after another is called to back up and take its load. Extreme cases are sent off on stretchers. The men generally make little or no ado, whatever their sufferings, — a few groans that cannot be repressed, and occasionally a scream of pain, as they lift a man into the ambulance.

"To-day, as I write, hundreds more are expected, and to-morrow and the next day more, and so on for many days.

"The soldiers are nearly all young men, and far more American than is generally supposed, — I should say nine tenths are native-born. Among the arrivals from Chancellorsville I find a large proportion of Ohio, Indiana, and Illinois men. As usual, there are all sorts of wounds. Some of the men are fearfully burnt from the explosion of artillery caissons. One ward has a long row of officers, some with ugly hurts. Yesterday was, perhaps, worse than usual. Amputations are going on, — the attendants are dressing wounds. As you pass by, you must be on your guard where you look. I saw, the other day, a gentleman — a visitor, apparently, from curiosity — in one of the wards stop and turn a moment to look at an awful wound they were probing, etc. He turned pale, and in a moment more he had fainted away and fallen on the floor."

An episode, — the death of a New York soldier: —

"This afternoon, July 22, 1863, I spent a long time with a young man I have been with a good deal from time to time, named Oscar F. Wilber, company G, 154th New York, low with chronic diarrhœa, and a bad wound also. He asked me to read him a chapter in the New Testament. I complied, and asked him what I should read. He said: 'Make your own choice.' I opened at the close of one of the first books of the Evangelists, and read

the chapters describing the latter hours of Christ
and the scenes at the crucifixion. The poor, wasted
young man asked me to read the following chapter
also, how Christ rose again. I read very slowly,
as Oscar was feeble. It pleased him very much,
yet the tears were in his eyes. He asked me if I
enjoyed religion. I said: 'Perhaps not, my dear,
in the way you mean, and yet, maybe, it is the
same thing.' He said: 'It is my chief reliance.'
He talked of death, and said he did not fear it. I
said: 'Why, Oscar, don't you think you will get
well?' He said: 'I may, but it is not probable.'
He spoke calmly of his condition. The wound was
very bad; it discharged much. Then the diarrhœa
had prostrated him, and I felt that he was even
then the same as dying. He behaved very manly
and affectionate. The kiss I gave him as I was
about leaving he returned fourfold. He gave me
his mother's address, Mrs. Sally D. Wilber, Alle-
ghany post-office, Cattaraugus County, New York.
I had several such interviews with him. He died
a few days after the one just described."

And here, also, a characteristic scene in another of
those long barracks: —

"It is Sunday afternoon (middle of summer,
1864), hot and oppressive, and very silent through
the ward. I am taking care of a critical case, now
lying in a half lethargy. Near where I sit is a
suffering rebel, from the 8th Louisiana; his name

is Irving. He has been here a long time, badly wounded, and has lately had his leg amputated. It is not doing very well. Right opposite me is a sick soldier boy, laid down with his clothes on, sleeping, looking much wasted, his pallid face on his arm. I see by the yellow trimming on his jacket that he is a cavalry boy. He looks so handsome as he sleeps, one must needs go nearer to him. I step softly over to him, and find by his card that he is named William Cone, of the 1st Maine Cavalry, and his folks live in Skowhegan."

In a letter to his mother in 1863 he says, in reference to his hospital services: "I have got in the way, after going lightly, as it were, all through the wards of a hospital, and trying to give a word of cheer, if nothing else, to every one, then confining my special attention to the few where the investment seems to tell best, and who want it most. . . . Mother, I have real pride in telling you that I have the consciousness of saving quite a number of lives by keeping the men from giving up, and being a good deal with them. The men say it is so, and the doctors say it is so; and I will candidly confess I can see it is true, though I say it myself. I know you will like to hear it, mother, so I tell you."

Again he says: "I go among the worst fevers and wounds with impunity; I go among the smallpox, etc., just the same. I feel to go without apprehension, and so I go: nobody else goes; but, as the darkey said there at Charleston when the boat ran on a flat and the rebel sharpshooters were peppering them, '*somebody* must jump in de water and shove de boat off.'"

In another letter to his mother he thus accounts for his effect upon the wounded soldiers: "I fancy the reason I am able to do some good in the hospitals among the poor, languishing, and wounded boys, is that I am so large and well, — indeed, like a great wild buffalo with much hair. Many of the soldiers are from the West and far North, and they like a man that has not the bleached, shiny, and shaved cut of the cities and the East."

As to Whitman's appearance about this time, we get an inkling from another letter to his mother, giving an account of an interview he had with Senator Preston King, to whom Whitman applied for assistance in procuring a clerkship in one of the departments. King said to him, "Why, how can I do this thing, or anything for you? How do I know but you are a secessionist? You look for all the world like an old Southern planter, — a regular Carolina or Virginia planter."

The great suffering of the soldiers and their heroic fortitude move him deeply. He says to his mother: "Nothing of ordinary misfortune seems as it used to, and death itself has lost all its terrors; I have seen so many cases in which it was so welcome

41

and such a relief." Again: "I go to the hospitals every day or night. I believe no men ever loved each other as I and some of these poor wounded, sick, and dying men love each other."

Whitman's services in the hospitals began to tell seriously upon his health in June, 1864, when he had "spells of deathly faintness, and had trouble in the head." The doctors told him he must keep away for a while, but he could not. Under date of June 7, 1864, he writes to his mother: —

"There is a very horrible collection in Armory Building (in Armory Square Hospital), — about two hundred of the worst cases you ever saw, and I have probably been too much with them. It is enough to melt the heart of a stone. Over one third of them are amputation cases. Well, mother, poor Oscar Cunningham is gone at last (he is the 82d Ohio boy, wounded May 3, '63). I have written so much of him I suppose you feel as if you almost knew him. I was with him Saturday forenoon, and also evening. He was more composed than usual; could not articulate very well. He died about two o'clock Sunday morning, very easy, they told me. I was not there. It was a blessed relief. His life has been misery for months. I believe I told you, last letter, I was quite blue from the deaths of several of the poor young men I knew well, especially two of whom I had strong hopes of their getting up. Things are going pretty badly with the wounded. They are crowded here in Washington in immense numbers, and all those that came up from the Wilderness and that region arrived here so neglected and in such plight it was awful (those that were at Fredericksburg, and also from Belle Plain). The papers are full of puffs, etc., but the truth is the largest proportion of worst cases get little or no attention.

"We receive them here with their wounds full of worms, — some all swelled and inflamed. Many of the amputations have to be done over again. One new feature is, that many of the poor, afflicted young men are crazy; every ward has some in it that are wandering. They have suffered too much, and it is perhaps a privilege that they are out of their senses. Mother, it is most too much for a fellow, and I sometimes wish I was out of it; but I suppose it is because I have not felt firstrate myself."

Of the Ohio soldier above referred to, Whitman had written a few days before: "You remember I told you of him a year ago, when he was first brought in. I thought him the noblest specimen of a young Western man I had seen. A real giant in size, and always with a smile on his face. Oh, what a change! He has long been very irritable to every one but me, and his frame is all wasted away."

To his brother Jeff he wrote: "Of the many I have seen die, or known of the past year, I have not seen or known of one who met death with any terror.

43

Yesterday I spent a good part of the afternoon with a young man of seventeen named Charles Cutter, of Lawrence City, 1st Massachusetts Heavy Artillery, Battery M. He was brought into one of the hospitals mortally wounded in abdomen. Well, I thought to myself as I sat looking at him, it ought to be a relief to his folks, after all, if they could see how little he suffered. He lay very placid, in a half lethargy, with his eyes closed; it was very warm, and I sat a long while fanning him and wiping the sweat. At length he opened his eyes quite wide and clear, and looked inquiringly around. I said, ' What is it, my dear ? do you want anything ? ' He said quietly, with a good-natured smile, ' Oh, nothing; I was only looking around to see who was with me.' His mind was somewhat wandering, yet he lay so peaceful in his dying condition. He seemed to be a real New England country boy, so good-natured, with a pleasant, homely way, and quite fine-looking. Without any doubt, he died in course of the night."

Another extract from a letter to his mother in April, 1864: —

" Mother, you don't know what a feeling a man gets after being in the active sights and influences of the camp, the army, the wounded, etc. He gets to have a deep feeling he never experienced before, — the flag, the tune of ' Yankee Doodle,' and similar things produce an effect on a fellow never felt before. I have seen tears on the men's cheeks, and others turn pale under such circumstances. I have a little flag, — it belonged to one of our cavalry regiments, — presented to me by one of the wounded. It was taken by the rebs in a cavalry fight, and rescued by our men in a bloody little skirmish. It cost three men's lives just to get one little flag, four by three. Our men rescued it, and tore it from the breast of a dead rebel. All that just for the name of getting their little banner back again. The man that got it was very badly wounded, and they let him keep it. I was with him a good deal. He wanted to give me something, he said; he did not expect to live; so he gave me the little banner as a keepsake. I mention this, mother, to show you a specimen of the feeling. There is n't a regiment of cavalry or infantry that would n't do the same on occasion."

[An army surgeon, who at the time watched with curiosity Mr. Whitman's movements among the soldiers in the hospitals, has since told me that his principles of operation, effective as they were, seemed strangely few, simple, and on a low key, — to act upon the appetite, to cheer by a healthy and fitly bracing appearance and demeanor; and to fill and satisfy in certain cases the affectional longings of the patients, was about all. He carried among them no sentimentalism nor moralizing; spoke not to any man of his "sins," but gave something good

to eat, a buoying word, or a trifling gift and a look.
He appeared with ruddy face, clean dress, with a
flower or a green sprig in the lapel of his coat.
Crossing the fields in summer, he would gather a
great bunch of dandelion blossoms, and red and
white clover, to bring and scatter on the cots, as
reminders of out-door air and sunshine.

When practicable, he came to the long and
crowded wards of the maimed, the feeble, and the
dying, only after preparations as for a festival, —
strengthened by a good meal, rest, the bath, and
fresh underclothes. He entered with a huge haversack slung over his shoulder, full of appropriate
articles, with parcels under his arms, and protuber-
ant pockets. He would sometimes come in summer
with a good-sized basket filled with oranges, and
would go round for hours paring and dividing them
among the feverish and thirsty.]

Of his devotion to the wounded soldiers there are
many witnesses. A well-known correspondent of
the "New York Herald" writes thus about him in
April, 1876: —

"I first heard of him among the sufferers on
the Peninsula after a battle there. Subsequently I
saw him, time and again, in the Washington hospitals, or wending his way there, with basket or
haversack on his arm, and the strength of beneficence suffusing his face. His devotion surpassed
the devotion of woman. It would take a volume

to tell of his kindness, tenderness, and thoughtful-
ness.

"Never shall I forget one night when I accom-
panied him on his rounds through a hospital filled
with those wounded young Americans whose heroism he has sung in deathless numbers. There were
three rows of cots, and each cot bore its man.
When he appeared, in passing along, there was a
smile of affection and welcome on every face, however wan, and his presence seemed to light up the
place as it might be lighted by the presence of the
God of Love. From cot to cot they called him,
often in tremulous tones or in whispers; they embraced him; they touched his hand; they gazed at
him. To one he gave a few words of cheer; for another he wrote a letter home; to others he gave an
orange, a few comfits, a cigar, a pipe and tobacco, a
sheet of paper or a postage-stamp, all of which and
many other things were in his capacious haversack.
From another he would receive a dying message for
mother, wife, or sweetheart; for another he would
promise to go an errand; to another, some special
friend very low, he would give a manly farewell kiss.
He did the things for them no nurse or doctor
could do, and he seemed to leave a benediction at
every cot as he passed along. The lights had
gleamed for hours in the hospital that night before
he left it, and, as he took his way towards the door,
you could hear the voices of many a stricken hero

47

calling 'Walt, Walt, Walt! come again! come
again!'"

III

Out of that experience in camp and hospital the
pieces called "Drum-Taps," first published in 1865,
— since merged in his "Leaves," — were produced.
Their descriptions and pictures, therefore, come from
life. The vivid incidents of "The Dresser" are
but daguerreotypes of the poet's own actual movements among the bad cases of the wounded after a
battle. The same personal knowledge runs through
"A Sight in Camp in the Daybreak Gray and Dim,"
"Come up from the Fields, Father," etc., etc.

The reader of this section of Whitman's work
soon discovers that it is not the purpose of the poet
to portray battles and campaigns, or to celebrate
special leaders or military prowess, but rather to
chant the human aspects of anguish that follow in
the train of war. He perhaps feels that the permanent condition of modern society is that of peace;
that war as a business, as a means of growth, has
served its time; and that, notwithstanding the vast
difference between ancient and modern warfare,
both in the spirit and in the means, Homer's pictures are essentially true yet, and no additions to
them can be made. War can never be to us what
it has been to the nations of all ages down to the
present; never the main fact, the paramount con-

dition, tyrannizing over all the affairs of national and individual life, but only an episode, a passing interruption; and the poet, who in our day would be as true to his nation and times as Homer was to his, must treat of it from the standpoint of peace and progress, and even benevolence. Vast armies rise up in a night and disappear in a day; a million of men, inured to battle and to blood, go back to the avocations of peace without a moment's confusion or delay, — indicating clearly the tendency that prevails.

Apostrophizing the genius of America in the supreme hour of victory, he says: —

" No poem proud, I, chanting, bring to thee — nor mastery's rapturous verse :—
But a little book containing night's darkness and blood-dripping wounds,
And psalms of the dead."

The collection is also remarkable for the absence of all sectional or partisan feeling. Under the head of " Reconciliation " are these lines: —

" Word over all, beautiful as the sky!
Beautiful that war, and all its deeds of carnage, must in time be utterly lost!
That the hands of the sisters Death and Night incessantly, softly wash again, and ever again, this soil'd world ;
. . . For my enemy is dead — a man divine as myself is dead ;

49

I look where he lies, white-faced and still, in the coffin —
>   I draw near;
I bend down, and touch lightly with my lips the white
>   face in the coffin."

Perhaps the most noteworthy of Whitman's war poems is the one called "When Lilacs last in the Door-Yard bloomed," written in commemoration of President Lincoln.

The main effect of this poem is of strong, solemn, and varied music; and it involves in its construction a principle after which perhaps the great composers most work, — namely, spiritual auricular analogy. At first it would seem to defy analysis, so rapt is it, and so indirect. No reference whatever is made to the mere fact of Lincoln's death; the poet does not even dwell upon its unprovoked atrocity, and only occasionally is the tone that of lamentation; but, with the intuitions of the grand art, which is the most complex when it seems most simple, he seizes upon three beautiful facts of nature, which he weaves into a wreath for the dead President's tomb. The central thought is of death, but around this he curiously twines, first, the early-blooming lilacs which the poet may have plucked the day the dark shadow came; next the song of the hermit thrush, the most sweet and solemn of all our songsters, heard at twilight in the dusky cedars; and with these the evening star, which, as many may remember, night after night in the early part of that eventful spring, hung low in the west with unusual and tender brightness. These are the premises from which he starts his solemn chant.

The attitude, therefore, is not that of being bowed down and weeping hopeless tears, but of singing a commemorative hymn, in which the voices of nature join, and it fits that exalted condition of the soul which serious events and the presence of death induce. There are no words of mere eulogy, no statistics, and no story or narrative; but there are pictures, processions, and a strange mingling of darkness and light, of grief and triumph: now the voice of the bird, or the drooping lustrous star, or the sombre thought of death; then a recurrence to the open scenery of the land as it lay in the April light, "the summer approaching with richness and the fields all busy with labor," presently dashed in upon by a spectral vision of armies with torn and bloody battle-flags, and, again, of the white skeletons of young men long afterward strewing the ground. Hence the piece has little or nothing of the character of the usual productions on such occasions. It is dramatic; yet there is no development of plot, but a constant interplay, a turning and returning of images and sentiments.

The poet breaks a sprig of lilac from the bush in the door-yard, — the dark cloud falls on the land, — the long funeral sets out, — and then the apostrophe: —

"Coffin that passes through lanes and streets,
Through day and night, with the great cloud darkening
        the land,
With the pomp of the inloop'd flags, with the cities draped
        in black,
With the show of the States themselves, as of crape-veiled
        women, standing,
With processions long and winding, and the flambeaus
        of the night,
With the countless torches lit — with the silent sea of faces,
        and the unbared heads,
With the waiting depot, the arriving coffin, and the som-
        bre faces,
With dirges through the night, with the thousand voices
        rising strong and solemn;
With all the mournful voices of the dirges, pour'd around
        the coffin,
To dim-lit churches and the shuddering organs — Where
        amid these you journey,
With the tolling, tolling bells' perpetual clang;
Here! coffin that slowly passes,
I give you my sprig of lilac.

"(Nor for you, for one alone;
Blossoms and branches green to coffins all I bring;
For fresh as the morning — thus would I chant a song for
        you, O sane and sacred death.

"All over bouquets of roses,
O death! I cover you over with roses and early lilies;

But mostly and now the lilac that blooms the first,
Copious, I break, I break the sprigs from the bushes;]
With loaded arms I come, pouring for you,
For you and the coffins all of you, O death.)"

Then the strain goes on: —

"O how shall I warble myself for the dead one there I
    loved?
And how shall I deck my song for the large sweet soul that
    has gone?
And what shall my perfume be, for the grave of him I love?

"Sea-winds, blown from east and west,
Blown from the eastern sea, and blown from the western
    sea, till there on the prairies meeting:
These, and with these, and the breath of my chant,
I perfume the grave of him I love."

The poem reaches, perhaps, its height in the
matchless invocation to Death: —

"Come, lovely and soothing Death,
Undulate round the world, serenely arriving, arriving,
In the day, in the night, to all, to each,
Sooner or later, delicate Death.

"Prais'd be the fathomless universe,
For life and joy, and for objects and knowledge curious;
And for love, sweet love — but praise! O praise and
    praise,
For the sure-enwinding arms of cool-enfolding Death.

53

"Dark Mother, always gliding near, with soft feet,
Have none chanted for thee a chant of fullest welcome?
Then I chant it for thee — I glorify thee above all;
I bring thee a song that when thou must indeed come,
      come unfalteringly.

"Approach, encompassing Death — strong Deliveress!
When it is so — when thou hast taken them, I joyously
      sing the dead,
Lost in the loving, floating ocean of thee,
Laved in the flood of thy bliss, O Death.

"From me to thee glad serenades,
Dances for thee I propose, saluting thee — adornments
      and feastings for thee;
And the sights of the open landscape, and the high-spread
      sky are fitting,
And life and the fields, and the huge and thoughtful night.
The night, in silence, under many a star;
The ocean shore, and the husky whispering wave, whose
      voice I know;
And the soul turning to thee, O vast and well-veil'd Death,
And the body gratefully nestling close to thee."

IV

Whitman despised riches, and all mere worldly
success, as heartily as ever did any of the old Chris-
tians. All outward show and finery were intensely
distasteful to him. He probably would not have
accepted the finest house in New York on condition

that he live in it. During his hospital experiences
he cherished the purpose, as soon as the war was
over, of returning to Brooklyn, buying an acre or
two of land in some by-place on Long Island, and
building for himself and his family a cheap house.
When his brother Jeff contemplated building, he
advised him to build merely an Irish shanty. After
what he had seen the soldiers put up with, he
thought anything was good enough for him or his
people. In one of his letters to his mother, he
comments upon the un-American and inappropriate
ornamentation of the rooms in the Capitol building,
"without grandeur and without simplicity," he says.
In the state the country was in, and with the hospital scenes before him, the " poppy-show goddesses "
and the Italian style of decoration, etc., sickened
him, and he got away from it all as quickly as he
could.

v

During the war and after, I used to see a good
deal of Whitman in Washington. Summer and winter he was a conspicuous figure on Pennsylvania Avenue, where he was wont to walk for exercise and to
feed his hunger for faces. One would see him afar off,
in the crowd but not of it, — a large, slow-moving
figure, clad in gray, with broad-brimmed hat and
gray beard, — or, quite as frequently, on the front
platform of the street horse-cars with the driver.
My eye used to single him out many blocks away.

There were times during this period when his aspect was rather forbidding, — the physical man was too pronounced on first glance; the other man was hidden beneath the broad-brimmed hat. One needed to see the superbly domed head and classic brow crowning the rank physical man.

In his middle manhood, judging from the photos, he had a hirsute, kindly look, but very far removed from the finely cut traditional poet's face.

VI

I have often heard Whitman say that he inherited most excellent blood from his mother, — the old Dutch Van Velser strain, — Long Island blood filtered and vitalized through generations by the breath of the sea. He was his mother's child unmistakably. With all his rank masculinity, there was a curious feminine undertone in him which revealed itself in the quality of his voice, the delicate texture of his skin, the gentleness of his touch and ways, the attraction he had for children and the common people. A lady in the West, writing to me about him, spoke of his "great mother-nature." He was receptive, sympathetic, tender, and met you, not in a positive, aggressive manner, but more or less in a passive or neutral mood. He did not give his friends merely his mind, he gave them himself. It is not merely his mind or intellect that he has put into his poems, it is himself. Indeed, this

BIOGRAPHICAL AND PERSONAL

feminine mood or attitude might be dwelt upon at much length in considering his poems, — their solvent, absorbing power, and the way they yield themselves to diverse interpretations.

The sea, too, had laid its hand upon him, as I have already suggested. He never appeared so striking and impressive as when seen upon the beach. His large and tall gray figure looked at home, and was at home, upon the shore. The simple, strong, flowing lines of his face, his always clean fresh air, his blue absorbing eye, his commanding presence, and something pristine and elemental in his whole expression, seemed at once to put him *en rapport* with the sea. No phase of nature seems to have impressed him so deeply as the sea, or recurs so often in his poems.

VII

Whitman was preëminently manly, — richly endowed with the universal, healthy human qualities and attributes. Mr. Conway relates that when Emerson handed him the first thin quarto edition of "Leaves of Grass," while he was calling at his house in Concord, soon after the book appeared, he said, "Americans abroad may now come home: unto us a man is born."

President Lincoln, standing one day during the war before a window in the White House, saw Whitman slowly saunter by. He followed him with his eyes, and, turning, said to those about him, "Well, *he* looks like a *man*."

" Meeter of savage and gentleman on equal terms."

During Whitman's Western tour in 1879 or '80, at some point in Kansas, in company with several well-known politicians and government officials, he visited a lot of Indians who were being held as prisoners. The sheriff told the Indians who the distinguished men were who were about to see them, but the Indians paid little attention to them as, one after the other, the officials and editors passed by them. Behind all came Whitman. The old chief looked at him steadily, then extended his hand and said, "How!" All the other Indians followed, surrounding Whitman, shaking his hand and making the air melodious with their "Hows." The incident evidently pleased the old poet a good deal.

VIII

Whitman was of large mould in every way, and of bold, far-reaching schemes, and is very sure to fare better at the hands of large men than of small. The first and last impression which his personal presence always made upon one was of a nature wonderfully gentle, tender, and benignant. His culture, his intellect, was completely suffused and dominated by his humanity, so that the impression you got from him was not that of a learned or a literary person, but of fresh, strong, sympathetic human nature, — such an impression, I fancy, only fuller, as one might have got from Walter Scott. This was perhaps the secret of the attraction he had for the common, unlettered people and for children. I think that even his literary friends often sought his presence less for conversation than to bask in his physical or psychical sunshine, and to rest upon his boundless charity. The great service he rendered to the wounded and homesick soldiers in the hospitals during the war came from his copious endowment of this broad, sweet, tender democratic nature. He brought father and mother to them, and the tonic and cheering atmosphere of simple, affectionate home life.

In person Whitman was large and tall, above six feet, with a breezy, open-air look. His temperament was sanguine; his voice was a tender baritone. The dominant impression he made was that of something fresh and clean. I remember the first time I met him, which was in Washington, in the fall of 1863. 1 was impressed by the fine grain and clean, fresh quality of the man. Some passages in his poems had led me to expect something different. He always had the look of a man who had just taken a bath. The skin was light and clear, and the blood well to the surface. His body, as I once noticed when we were bathing in the surf, had a peculiar fresh bloom and fineness and

delicacy of texture. His physiology was undoubtedly remarkable, unique. The full beauty of his
face and head did not appear till he was past sixty.
After that, I have little doubt, it was the finest
head this age or country has seen. Every artist
who saw him was instantly filled with a keen desire
to sketch him. The lines were so simple, so free,
and so strong. High, arching brows; straight,
clear-cut nose; heavy-lidded blue-gray eyes; forehead not thrust out and emphasized, but a vital
part of a symmetrical, dome-shaped head; ear large,
and the most delicately carved I have ever seen;
the mouth and chin hidden by a soft, long, white
beard. It seems to me his face steadily refined
and strengthened with age. Time depleted him
in just the right way, — softened his beard and
took away the too florid look; subdued the carnal
man, and brought out more fully the spiritual
man. When I last saw him (December 26, 1891),
though he had been very near death for many days,
I am sure I had never seen his face so beautiful.
There was no breaking-down of the features, or the
least sign of decrepitude, such as we usually note in
old men. The expression was full of pathos, but it
was as grand as that of a god. I could not think
of him as near death, he looked so unconquered.

In Washington I knew Whitman intimately from
the fall of 1863 to the time he left in 1873. In
Camden I visited him yearly after that date, usu-

ally in the late summer or fall. I will give one
glimpse of him from my diary, under date of
August 18, 1887. I reached his house in the morning, before he was up. Presently he came slowly
downstairs and greeted me. "Find him pretty
well, — looking better than last year. With his
light-gray suit, and white hair, and fresh pink
face, he made a fine picture. Among other things,
we talked of the Swinburne attack (then recently
published). W. did not show the least feeling on
the subject, and, I clearly saw, was absolutely un-
disturbed by the article. I told him I had always
been more disturbed by S.'s admiration for him than
I was now by his condemnation. By and by W. had
his horse hitched up, and we started for Glendale,
ten miles distant, to see young Gilchrist, the artist.
A fine drive through a level farming and truck-
gardening country; warm, but breezy. W. drives
briskly, and salutes every person we meet, little
and big, black and white, male and female. Nearly
all return his salute cordially. He said he knew
but few of those he spoke to, but that, as he grew
older, the old Long Island custom of his people,
to speak to every one on the road, was strong
upon him. One tipsy man in a buggy responded,
'Why, pap, how d' ye do, pap?' We talked of
many things. I recall this remark of W., as something I had not before thought of, that it was difficult to see what the old feudal world would have

come to without Christianity: it would have been like a body acted upon by the centrifugal force without the centripetal. Those haughty lords and chieftains needed the force of Christianity to check and curb them, etc. W. knew the history of many prominent houses on the road: here a crazy man lived, with two colored men to look after him; there, in that fine house among the trees, an old maid, who had spent a large fortune on her house and lands, and was now destitute, yet she was a woman of remarkable good sense. We returned to Camden before dark, W. apparently not fatigued by the drive of twenty miles."

In death what struck me most about the face was its perfect symmetry. It was such a face, said Mr. Conway, as Rembrandt would have selected from a million. "It is the face of an aged loving child. As I looked, it was with the reflection that, during an acquaintance of thirty-six years, I never heard from those lips a word of irritation, or depreciation of any being. I do not believe that Buddha, of whom he appeared an avatar, was more gentle to all men, women, children, and living things."

IX

For one of the best pen-sketches of Whitman in his old age we are indebted to Dr. J. Johnston, a young Scotch physician of Bolton, England, who visited Whitman in the summer of 1890. I quote from a little pamphlet which the doctor printed on his return home: —

"The first thing about himself that struck me was the physical immensity and magnificent proportions of the man, and, next, the picturesque majesty of his presence as a whole.

"He sat quite erect in a great cane-runged chair, cross-legged, and clad in rough gray clothes, with slippers on his feet, and a shirt of pure white linen, with a great wide collar edged with white lace, the shirt buttoned about midway down his breast, the big lapels of the collar thrown open, the points touching his shoulders, and exposing the upper portion of his hirsute chest. He wore a vest of gray homespun, but it was unbuttoned almost to the bottom. He had no coat on, and his shirt sleeves were turned up above the elbows, exposing most beautifully shaped arms, and flesh of the most delicate whiteness. Although it was so hot, he did not perspire visibly, while I had to keep mopping my face. His hands are large and massive, but in perfect proportion to the arms; the fingers long, strong, white, and tapering to a blunt end. His nails are square, showing about an eighth of an inch separate from the flesh, and I noticed that there was not a particle of impurity beneath any of them. But his majesty is concentrated in his head, which is set with leonine grace and dignity upon his broad, square shoulders; and it is almost entirely covered with long, fine, straggling hair, silvery and glistening, pure and white as sunlit snow, rather thin on the top of his high, rounded crown, streaming over and around his large but delicately-shaped ears, down the back of his big neck; and, from his pinky-white cheeks and top lip, over the lower part of his face, right down to the middle of his chest, like a cataract of materialized, white, glistening vapor, giving him a most venerable and patriarchal appearance. His high, massive forehead is seamed with wrinkles. His nose is large, strong, broad, and prominent, but beautifully chiseled and proportioned, almost straight, very slightly depressed at the tip, and with deep furrows on each side, running down to the angles of the mouth. The eyebrows are thick and shaggy, with strong, white hair, very highly arched and standing a long way above the eyes, which are of a light blue with a tinge of gray, small, rather deeply set, calm, clear, penetrating, and revealing unfathomable depths of tenderness, kindness, and sympathy. The upper eyelids droop considerably over the eyeballs. The lips, which are partly hidden by the thick, white mustache, are full. The whole face impresses one with a sense of resoluteness, strength, and intellectual power, and yet withal a winning sweetness, unconquerable radiance, and hopeful joyousness. His voice is highly pitched and musical, with a timbre which is astonishing in an old man. There is none of the tremor, quaver, or shrillness usually observed in them, but his utterance is clear, ringing, and most sweetly musical. But it was not in any one of these features that his charm lay so much as in his *tout ensemble*, and the irresistible magnetism of his sweet, aromatic presence, which seemed to exhale sanity, purity, and naturalness, and exercised over me an attraction which positively astonished me, producing an exaltation of mind and soul which no man's presence ever did before. I felt that I was here face to face with the living embodiment of all that was good, noble, and lovable in humanity."

x

British critics have spoken of Whitman's athleticism, his athletic temperament, etc., but he was in no sense a muscular man, an athlete. His body, though superb, was curiously the body of a child; one saw this in its form, in its pink color, and in the delicate texture of the skin. He took little interest in feats of strength or in athletic sports. He walked with a slow, rolling gait, indeed, moved slowly in all ways; he always had an air of infinite leisure. For several years, while a clerk in the Attorney-General's Office in Washington, his exercise for an hour each day consisted in tossing a few feet into the air, as he walked, a round, smooth stone, of about one pound weight, and catching it as it fell. Later in life, and after his first paralytic stroke, when in the woods, he liked to bend down the young saplings, and exercise his arms and chest in that way. In his poems much emphasis is laid upon health, and upon purity and sweetness of body, but none upon mere brute strength. This is what he says "To a Pupil:" —

1. Is reform needed? Is it through you?
   The greater the reform needed, the greater the PERSONALITY you need to accomplish it.

2. You! do you not see how it would serve to have eyes, blood, complexion, clean and sweet?
   Do you not see how it would serve to have such a body and Soul, that when you enter the crowd, an atmosphere of desire and command enters with you, and every one is impressed with your personality?

3. O the magnet! the flesh over and over!
   Go, mon cher! if need be, give up all else, and commence to-day to inure yourself to pluck, reality, self-esteem, definiteness, elevatedness,
   Rest not, till you rivet and publish yourself of your own personality.

It is worthy of note that Whitman's Washington physician said he had one of the most thoroughly natural physical systems he had ever known, — the freest, probably, from extremes or any disproportion; which answers to the perfect sanity which all his friends must have felt with regard to his mind.

A few years ago a young English artist stopping in this country made several studies of him. In one of them which he showed me, he had left the face blank, but had drawn the figure from the head down with much care. It was so expressive, so unmistakably Whitman, conveyed so surely a certain majesty and impressiveness that pertained to the poet physically, that I looked upon it with no ordinary interest. Every wrinkle in the garments seemed to proclaim the man. Probably a similar painting of any of one's friends would be more or less a recognizable portrait, but I doubt if it would speak so emphatically as did this incomplete sketch. I thought it all the more significant in this case because Whitman laid such stress upon the human body in his poems, built so extensively upon it, curiously identifying it with the soul, and declaring his belief that if he made the poems of his body and of mortality he would thus supply himself with the poems of the soul and of immortality. "Behold," he says, "the body includes and is the meaning, the main concern, and includes and is the soul; whoever you are, how superb and how divine is your body, or any part of it!" He runs this physiological thread all through his book, and strings upon it many valuable lessons and many noble sentiments. Those who knew him well, I think, will agree with me that his bodily presence was singularly magnetic, restful, and positive, and that it furnished a curious and suggestive commentary upon much there is in his poetry.

The Greeks, who made so much more of the human body than we do, seem not to have carried so much meaning, so much history, in their faces as does the modern man; the soul was not concentrated here, but was more evenly distributed over the whole body. Their faces expressed repose, harmony, power of command. I think Whitman was like the Greeks in this respect. His face had none of the eagerness, sharpness, nervousness, of the modern face. It had but few lines, and these were Greek. From the mouth up, the face was expressive of Greek purity, simplicity, strength, and repose. The mouth was large and loose, and expressive of another side of his nature. It was a mouth that required the check and curb of that classic brow.

And the influence of his poems is always on the side of physiological cleanliness and strength, and severance from all that corrupts and makes morbid and mean. He says the "expression of a well-made man appears not only in his face: it is in his limbs and joints also; it is curiously in the joints of his hips and wrists; it is in his walk, the carriage of his neck, the flex of his waist and knees; dress does not hide him; the strong, sweet, supple quality he has strikes through the cotton and flannel; to see him pass conveys as much as the best poem, perhaps more. You linger to see his back, and the back of his neck and shoulder-side." He says he has perceived that to be with those he likes is enough: "To be surrounded by beautiful, curious, breathing, laughing flesh is enough, — I do not ask any more delight; I swim in it, as in a sea. There is something in staying close to men and women and looking on them, and in the contact and odor of them, that pleases the soul well. All things please the soul, but these please the soul well." Emerson once asked Whitman what it was he found in the society of the common people that satisfied him so; for his part, he could not find anything. The subordination by Whitman of the purely intellectual to the human and physical, which runs all through his poems and is one source of their power, Emerson, who was deficient in the sensuous, probably could not appreciate.

XI

The atmosphere of Whitman personally was that of a large, tolerant, tender, sympathetic, restful man, easy of approach, indifferent to any special social or other distinctions and accomplishments that might be yours, and regarding you from the start for yourself alone.

Children were very fond of him; and women, unless they had been prejudiced against him, were

strongly drawn toward him. His personal magnetism was very great, and was warming and cheering. He was rich in temperament, probably beyond any other man of his generation, — rich in all
the purely human and emotional endowments and
basic qualities. Then there was a look about him
hard to describe, and which I have seen in no other
face, — a gray, brooding, elemental look, like the
granite rock, something primitive and Adamic that
might have belonged to the first man; or was it a
suggestion of the gray, eternal sea that he so loved,
near which he was born, and that had surely set its
seal upon him? I know not, but I feel the man
with that look is not of the day merely, but of the
centuries. His eye was not piercing, but absorbing, — "draining" is the word happily used by William O'Connor; the soul back of it drew things to
himself, and entered and possessed them through
sympathy and personal force and magnetism, rather
than through mere intellectual force.

XII

Walt Whitman was of the people, the common
people, and always gave out their quality and atmosphere. His commonness, his nearness, as of
the things you have always known, — the day, the
sky, the soil, your own parents, — were in no way
veiled, or kept in abeyance, by his culture or poetic
gifts. He was redolent of the human and the fa-

70

miliar. Though capable, on occasions, of great pride and hauteur, yet his habitual mood and presence was that of simple, average, healthful humanity, — the virtue and flavor of sailors, soldiers, laborers, travelers, or people who live with real things in the open air. His commonness rose into the uncommon, the extraordinary, but without any hint of the exclusive or specially favored. He was indeed "no sentimentalist, no stander above men and women or apart from them."

The spirit that animates every page of his book, and that it always effuses, is the spirit of common, universal humanity, — humanity apart from creeds, schools, conventions, from all special privileges and refinements, as it is in and of itself in its relations to the whole system of things, in contradistinction to the literature of culture which effuses the spirit of the select and exclusive.

His life was the same. Walt Whitman never stood apart from or above any human being. The common people — workingmen, the poor, the illiterate, the outcast — saw themselves in him, and he saw himself in them : the attraction was mutual. He was always content with common, unadorned humanity. Specially intellectual people rather repelled him; the wit, the scholar, the poet, must have a rich endowment of the common, universal, human attributes and qualities to pass current with him. He sought the society of boatmen, railroad men, farmers, mechanics, printers, teamsters, mothers of families, rather than the society of professional men or scholars. Men who had the quality of things in the open air — the virtue of rocks, trees, hills — drew him most; and it is these qualities and virtues that he has aimed above all others to put into his poetry, and to put them there in such a way that he who reads must feel and imbibe them.

The recognized poets put into their pages the virtue and quality of the fine gentleman, or of the sensitive, artistic nature: this poet of democracy effuses the atmosphere of fresh, strong Adamic man, — man acted upon at first hand by the shows and forces of universal nature.

If our poet ever sounds the note of the crude, the loud, the exaggerated, he is false to himself and to his high aims. I think he may be charged with having done so a few times, in his earlier work, but not in his later. In the 1860 edition of his poems stands this portraiture, which may stand for himself, with one or two features rather overdrawn: —

"His shape arises
Arrogant, masculine, naïve, rowdyish,
Laugher, weeper, worker, idler, citizen, countryman,
Saunterer of woods, stander upon hills, summer swimmer
      in rivers or by the sea,
Of pure American breed, of reckless health, his body per-
      fect, free from taint from top to toe, free forever
      from headache and dyspepsia, clean-breathed,

BIOGRAPHICAL AND PERSONAL

Ample-limbed, a good feeder, weight a hundred and eighty
pounds, full-blooded, six feet high, forty inches
round the breast and back,

Countenance sunburnt, bearded, calm, unrefined,

Reminder of animals, meeter of savage and gentleman on
equal terms,

Attitudes lithe and erect, costume free, neck gray and open,
of slow movement on foot,

Passer of his right arm round the shoulders of his friends,
companion of the street,

Persuader always of people to give him their sweetest
touches, and never their meanest.

A Manhattanese bred, fond of Brooklyn, fond of Broadway, fond of the life of the wharves and the great
ferries,

Enterer everywhere, welcomed everywhere, easily understood after all,

Never offering others, always offering himself, corroborating his phrenology,

Voluptuous, inhabitive, combative, conscientious, alimen-
tive, intuitive, of copious friendship, sublimity,
firmness, self-esteem, comparison, individuality,
form, locality, eventuality,

Avowing by life, manners, words to contribute illustrations of results of These States,

Teacher of the unquenchable creed namely egotism,

Inviter of others continually henceforth to try their
strength against his."

73

XIII

Whitman was determined, at whatever risk to his own reputation, to make the character which he has exploited in his poems a faithful compend of American humanity, and to do this the rowdy element could not be entirely ignored. Hence he unflinchingly imputes it to himself, as, for that matter, he has nearly every sin and dereliction mankind are guilty of.

Whitman developed slowly and late upon the side that related him to social custom and usage, — to the many fictions, concealments, make-believes, and subterfuges of the world of parlors and drawing-rooms. He never was an adept in what is called "good form;" the natural man that he was shows crude in certain relations. His publication of Emerson's letter with its magnificent eulogium of "Leaves of Grass" has been much commented upon. There may be two opinions as to the propriety of his course in this respect: a letter from a stranger upon a matter of public interest is not usually looked upon as a private letter. Emerson never spoke with more felicity and penetration than he does in this letter; but it is for Whitman's own sake that we would have had him practice self-denial in the matter; he greatly plumed himself upon Emerson's indorsement, and was guilty of the very bad taste of printing a sentence from the letter upon the cover of the next edition of his book. Grant that it showed a certain crudeness, unripeness, in one side of the man; later in life, he could not have erred in this way. Ruskin is reported saying that he never in his life wrote a letter to any human being that he would not be willing should be posted up in the market-place or cried by the public crier through the town. But Emerson was a much more timid and conforming man than Ruskin, and was much more likely to be shocked by such a circumstance.

It has been said that the publication of this letter much annoyed Emerson, and that he never forgave Whitman the offense. That he was disturbed by it and by the storm that arose there can be little doubt; but there is no evidence that he allowed the fact to interfere with his friendship for the poet. Charles W. Eldridge, who personally knew of the relations of the two men, says: —

"There was not a year from 1855 (the date of the Emerson letter and its publication) down to 1860 (the year Walt came to Boston to supervise the issue of the Thayer & Eldridge edition of 'Leaves of Grass'), that Emerson did not personally seek out Walt at his Brooklyn home, usually that they might have a long symposium together at the Astor House in New York. Besides that, during these years Emerson sent many of his closest friends, including Alcott and Thoreau, to see Walt, giving

them letters of introduction to him. This is not
the treatment usually accorded a man who has com-
mitted an unpardonable offense.

"I know that afterwards, during Walt's stay in
Boston, Emerson frequently came down from Concord to see him, and that they had many walks
and talks together, these conferences usually ending
with a dinner at the American House, at that time
Emerson's favorite Boston hotel. On several occasions they met by appointment in our counting-
room. Their relations were as cordial and friendly
as possible, and it was always Emerson who sought
out Walt, and never the other way, although, of
course, Walt appreciated and enjoyed Emerson's
companionship very much. In truth, Walt never
sought the company of notables at all, and was
always very shy of purely literary society. I know
that at this time Walt was invited by Emerson to
Concord, but declined to go, probably through his
fear that he would see too much of the literary
coterie that then clustered there, chiefly around
Emerson."

XIV

Whitman gave himself to men as men and not as
scholars or poets, and gave himself purely as a man.
While not specially averse to meeting people on
literary or intellectual grounds, yet it was more to
his taste to meet on the broadest, commonest, human

Boston, Sept: 24 1881

Dear friend

Yours rec'd — I am now back here finishing up — only staid a few days in Concord, but they were mark'd days. Sunday, Emerson & his wife, son Edward & wife &c. gave me a dinner — two hours — every thing just right every way — a dozen people there (the family & relatives) — for my part I thought the old man in his smilarity and alert quietude & withdrawnness & more eloquent *(he has a good color in his face & ate just as much dinner as any body)* grand, appropriate & impressive than ever — more indeed than could be described — Is n't it comforting that I have had — in the sunset as it were — so many significant affectionate hours with him under such quiet, beautiful, appropriate circumstances?

The books is done & will be in the market in a month or so — all about it has proceeded satisfactorily & I have had my own way in every thing — the old name "Leaves of Grass" is retained —it will be a †2 book —

— I shall probably go on to New York in about a week — shall stay at Johnston's, (address me there Mott avenue & 149th street N Y city) about a week or ten days — Besides this general death-gloom of the nation — have you heard of the sudden & dreadful death of our young friend Beatrice Gilchrist in performing some chemical experiment with ether? Joaquin Miller is here — is with me every day — Longfellow has been to see me — I have met O W Holmes & old Mr James. With love Walt Whitman grounds. What you had seen or felt or suffered or done was of much more interest to him than what you had read or thought; your speculation about the soul interested him less than the last person you had met, or the last chore you had done.

Any glimpse of the farm, the shop, the household — any bit of real life, anything that carried the flavor and quality of concrete reality — was very welcome to him; herein, no doubt, showing the healthy, objective, artist mind. He never tired of hearing me talk about the birds or wild animals, or my experiences in camp in the woods, the kind of characters I had met there, and the flavor of the life of remote settlements in Maine or Canada. His inward, subjective life was ample of itself; he was familiar with all your thoughts and speculations beforehand: what he craved was wider experience, — to see what you had seen, and feel what you had felt. He was fond of talking with returned travelers and explorers, and with sailors, soldiers, mechanics; much of his vast stores of information upon all manner of subjects was acquired at first-hand, in the old way, from the persons who had seen or done or been what they described or related.

He had almost a passion for simple, unlettered humanity, — an attraction which specially intellectual persons will hardly understand. Schooling and culture are so often purchased at such an expense to the innate, fundamental human qualities! Ignorance, with sound instincts and the quality which converse with real things imparts to men, was more acceptable to him than so much of our sophisticated knowledge, or our studied wit, or our artificial poetry.

XV

At the time of Whitman's death, one of our leading literary journals charged him with having brought on premature decay by leading a riotous and debauched life. I hardly need say that there was no truth in the charge. The tremendous emotional strain of writing his "Leaves," followed by his years of service in the army hospitals, where he contracted blood-poison, resulted at the age of fifty-four in the rupture of a small blood-vessel in the brain, which brought on partial paralysis. A sunstroke during his earlier manhood also played its part in the final break-down.

That, tried by the standard of the lives of our New England poets, Whitman's life was a blameless one, I do not assert; but that it was a sane, temperate, manly one, free from excesses, free from the perversions and morbidities of a mammonish, pampered, over-stimulated age, I do believe. Indeed, I may say I know. The one impression he never failed to make — physically, morally, intellectually — on young and old, women and men, was that of health, sanity, sweetness. This is the impression he

seems to have made upon Mr. Howells, when he
met the poet at Pfaff's early in the sixties.

The critic I have alluded to inferred license in
the man from liberty in the poet. He did not have
the gumption to see that Whitman made the experience of all men his own, and that his scheme included the evil as well as the good; that especially
did he exploit the unloosed, all-loving, all-accepting
natural man, — the man who is done with conventions, illusions, and all morbid pietisms, and who
gives himself lavishly to all that begets and sustains
life. Yet not the natural or carnal man for his own
sake, but for the sake of the spiritual meanings and
values to which he is the key. Indeed, Whitman is
about the most uncompromising spiritualist in literature; with him, all things exist by and for the soul.
He felt the tie of universal brotherhood, also, as
few have felt it. It was not a theory with him, but
a fact that shaped his life and colored his poems.
"Whoever degrades another degrades me," and the
thought fired his imagination.

XVI

The student of Whitman's life and works will be
early struck by three things, — his sudden burst
into song, the maturity of his work from the first,
and his self-knowledge and self-estimate. The fit
of inspiration came upon him suddenly; it was like
the flowering of the orchards in spring; there was

little or no hint of it till almost the very hour of the event. Up to the time of the appearance of the first edition of "Leaves of Grass," he had produced nothing above mediocrity. A hack writer on newspapers and magazines, then a carpenter and house-builder in a small way, then that astounding revelation "Leaves of Grass," the very audacity of it a gospel in itself. How dare he do it? how could he do it, and not betray hesitation or self-consciousness? It is one of the exceptional events in literary history. The main body of his work was produced in five or six years, or between 1854 and 1859. Of course it was a sudden flowering, which, consciously or unconsciously, must have been long preparing in his mind. His work must have had a long foreground, as Emerson suggested. Dr. Bucke, his biographer, thinks it was a special inspiration, — something analogous to Paul's conversion, a sudden opening of what the doctor calls "cosmic consciousness."

Another student and lover of Whitman says: "It is certain that some time about his thirty-fifth year [probably a little earlier] there came over him a decided change: he seemed immensely to broaden and deepen; he became less interested in what are usually regarded as the more practical affairs of life. He lost what little ambition he ever had for money-making, and permitted good business opportunities to pass unheeded. He ceased to write the somewhat interesting but altogether commonplace and respectable stories and verses which he had been in the habit of contributing to periodicals. He would take long trips into the country, no one knew where, and would spend more time in his favorite haunts about the city, or on the ferries, or the tops of omnibuses, at the theatre and opera, in picture galleries, and wherever he could observe men and women and art and nature."

Then the maturity of his work from the first line of it! It seems as if he came into the full possession of himself and of his material at one bound, — never had to grope for his way and experiment, as most men do. What apprenticeship he served, or with whom he served it, we get no hint. He has come to his own, and is in easy, joyful possession of it, when he first comes into view. He outlines his scheme in his first poem, "Starting from Paumanok," and he has kept the letter and the spirit of every promise therein made. We never see him doubtful or hesitating; we never see him battling for his territory, and uncertain whether or not he is upon his own ground. He has an air of contentment, of mastery and triumph, from the start.

His extraordinary self-estimate and self-awareness are equally noticeable. We should probably have to go back to sacred history to find a parallel case. The manner of man he was, his composite character, his relation to his country and times, his unlikeness to other poets, his affinity to the common people, how he would puzzle and elude his critics, how his words would itch at our ears till we understood them, etc., — how did he know all this from the first?

HIS RULING IDEAS AND AIMS

I

LET me here summarize some of the ideas and principles in which "Leaves of Grass" has its root, and from which it starts. A collection of poems in the usual sense, a variety of themes artistically treated and appealing to our æsthetic perceptibilities alone, it is not. It has, strictly speaking, but one theme, — personality, the personality of the poet himself. To exploit this is always the main purpose, and, in doing so, to make the book both directly and indirectly a large, impassioned utterance upon all the main problems of life and of nationality. It is primitive, like the early literature of a race or people, in that its spirit and purpose are essentially religious. It is like the primitive literatures also in its prophetic cry and in its bardic simplicity and homeliness, and unlike them in its faith and joy and its unconquerable optimism.

It has been not inaptly called the bible of democracy. Its biblical features are obvious enough with the darker negative traits left out. It is Israel with science and the modern added.

Whitman was swayed by a few great passions, — the passion for country, the passion for comrades, the cosmic passion, etc. His first concern seems always to have been for his country. He has touched no theme, named no man, not related in some way to America. The thought of it possessed him as thoroughly as the thought of Israel possessed the old Hebrew prophets. Indeed, it is the same passion, and flames up with the same vitality and power, — the same passion for race and nativity enlightened by science and suffused with the modern humanitarian spirit. Israel was exclusive and cruel. Democracy, as exemplified in Walt Whitman, is compassionate and all-inclusive: —

"My spirit has passed in compassion and determination
    around the whole earth,
I have looked for equals and lovers, and found them ready
    for me in all lands;
I think some divine rapport has equalized me with them.

"O vapors! I think I have risen with you, and moved
    away to distant continents, and fallen down there,
    for reasons,
I think I have blown with you, O winds,
O waters, I have fingered every shore with you."

II

The work springs from the modern democratic conception of society, — of absolute social equality.

It embodies the modern scientific conception of the universe, as distinguished from the old theological conception, — namely, that creation is good and sound in all its parts.

It embodies a conception of evil as a part of the good, of death as the friend and not the enemy of life.

It places comradeship, manly attachment, above sex love, and indicates it as the cement of future states and republics.

It makes the woman the equal of the man, his mate and not his toy.

It treats sexuality as a matter too vital and important to be ignored or trifled with, much less perverted or denied. A full and normal sexuality, — upon this the race stands. We pervert, we deny, we corrupt sex at our peril. Its perversions and abnormalities are to be remedied by a frank and fervent recognition of it, almost a new Priapic cult.

It springs from a conception of poetry quite different from the current conception. It aims at the poetry of things rather than of words, and works by suggestion and indirection rather than by elaboration.

It aims to project into literature a conception of the new democratic man, — a type larger, more copious, more candid, more religious, than we have been used to. It finds its ideals, not among scholars or in the parlor or counting-houses, but among workers, doers, farmers, mechanics, the heroes of land and sea.

Hence the atmosphere which it breathes and effuses is that of real things, real men and women. It has not the perfume of the distilled and concentrated, but the all but impalpable odor of the open air, the shore, the wood, the hilltop. It aims, not to be a book, but to be a man.

Its purpose is to stimulate and arouse, rather than to soothe and satisfy. It addresses the character, the intuitions, the ego, more than the intellect or the purely æsthetic faculties. Its end is not taste, but growth in the manly virtues and powers.

Its religion shows no trace of theology, or the conventional pietism.

It aspires to a candor and a directness like that of Nature herself.

It aims to let Nature speak without check, with original energy. The only checks are those which health and wholeness demand.

Its standards are those of the natural universal.

Its method is egocentric. The poet never goes out of himself, but draws everything into himself and makes it all serve to illustrate his personality.

Its form is not what is called artistic. Its suggestion is to be found in organic nature, in trees, clouds, and in the vital and flowing currents.

In its composition the author was doubtless greatly influenced by the opera and the great singers, and the music of the great composers. He would let himself go in the same manner and seek his effects through multitude and the quality of the living voice.

Finally, "Leaves of Grass" is an utterance out of the depths of primordial, aboriginal human nature. It embodies and exploits a character not rendered anæmic by civilization, but preserving a sweet and sane savagery, indebted to culture only as a means to escape culture, reaching back always, through books, art, civilization, to fresh, unsophisticated nature, and drawing his strength from this source.

Another of the ideas that master Whitman and rule him is the idea of identity, — that you are you and I am I, and that we are henceforth secure whatever comes or goes. He revels in this idea; it is fruitful with him; it begets in him the ego-enthusiasm, and is at the bottom of his unshakable faith in immortality. It leavens all his work. It cannot be too often said that the book is not merely a collection of pretty poems, themes elaborated and followed out at long removes from the personality of the poet, but a series of *sorties* into the world of materials, the American world, piercing through the ostensible shows of things to the interior meanings, and illustrating in a free and large way the genesis and growth of a man, his free use of the world about him, appropriating it to himself, seeking his spiritual identity through its various objects and experi-

ences, and giving in many direct and indirect ways
the meaning and satisfaction of life. There is much
in it that is not poetical in the popular sense, much
that is neutral and negative, and yet is an integral
part of the whole, as is the case in the world we
inhabit. If it offends, it is in a wholesome way,
like objects in the open air.

III

Whitman rarely celebrates exceptional characters. He loves the common humanity, and finds
his ideals among the masses. It is not difficult to
reconcile his attraction toward the average man,
towards workingmen and "powerful, uneducated
persons," with the ideal of a high excellence, because he finally rests only upon the most elevated
and heroic personal qualities, — elevated but well
grounded in the common and universal.

The types upon which he dwells the most fondly
are of the common people.

"I knew a man,
He was a common farmer — he was the father of five sons,
And in them were the fathers of sons — and in them were
　　　the fathers of sons.

"This man was of wonderful vigor, calmness, beauty of
　　　person,
The shape of his head, the richness and breadth of his
　　　manners, the pale yellow and white of his hair and

beard, and the immeasurable meaning of his black
eyes,

These I used to go and visit him to see — he was wise also,

He was six feet tall, he was over eighty years old —
his sons were massive, clean, bearded, tan-faced,
handsome,

They and his daughters loved him — all who saw him
loved him,

They did not love him by allowance — they loved him
with personal love;

He drank water only — the blood showed like scarlet
through the clear-brown skin of his face,

He was a frequent gunner and fisher — he sailed his boat
himself — he had a fine one presented to him by a
ship-joiner — he had fowling-pieces presented to
him by men that loved him;

When he went with his five sons and many grandsons to
hunt or fish, you would pick him out as the most
beautiful and vigorous of the gang,

You would wish long and long to be with him — you
would wish to sit by him in the boat, that you and
he might touch each other."

All the *motifs* of his work are the near, the vital, the
universal; nothing curious, or subtle, or far-fetched.
His working ideas are democracy, equality, personality, nativity, health, sexuality, comradeship, self-
esteem, the purity of the body, the equality of
the sexes, etc. Out of them his work radiates.
They are the eyes with which it sees, the ears

with which it hears, the feet upon which it goes.
The poems are less like a statement, an argument,
an elucidation, and more like a look, a gesture, a
tone of voice.

"The word I myself put primarily for the description of them as they stand at last," says the author,
"is the word Suggestiveness."

"Leaves of Grass" requires a large perspective;
you must not get your face too near the book.
You must bring to it a magnanimity of spirit, — a
charity and faith equal to its own. Looked at too
closely, it often seems incoherent and meaningless;
draw off a little and let the figure come out. The
book is from first to last a most determined attempt,
on the part of a large, reflective, loving, magnetic,
rather primitive, thoroughly imaginative personality,
to descend upon the materialism of the nineteenth
century, and especially upon a new democratic nation now in full career upon this continent, with
such poetic fervor and enthusiasm as to lift and
fill it with the deepest meanings of the spirit and
disclose the order of universal nature. The poet
has taken shelter behind no precedent, or criticism,
or partiality whatever, but has squarely and lovingly faced the oceanic amplitude and movement of
the life of his times and land, and fused them in
his fervid humanity, and imbued them with deepest
poetic meanings. One of the most striking features
of the book is the adequacy and composure, even

joyousness and elation, of the poet in the presence
of the huge materialism and prosaic conditions of
our democratic era. He spreads himself over it all,
he accepts and absorbs it all, he rejects no part;
and his quality, his individuality, shines through
it all, as the sun through vapors. The least line,
or fragment of a line, is redolent of Walt Whitman.
It is never so much the theme treated as it is the
man exploited and illustrated. Walt Whitman
does not write poems, strictly speaking, — does not
take a bit of nature or life or character and chisel
and carve it into a beautiful image or object, or
polish and elaborate a thought, embodying it in
pleasing tropes and pictures. His purpose is rather
to show a towering, loving, composite personality
moving amid all sorts of materials, taking them up
but for a moment, disclosing new meanings and
suggestions in them, passing on, bestowing himself
upon whoever or whatever will accept him, tossing
hints and clews right and left, provoking and stimulating the thought and imagination of his reader,
but finishing nothing for him, leaving much to be
desired, much to be completed by him in his turn.

IV

The reader who would get at the spirit and meaning of "Leaves of Grass" must remember that its
animating principle, from first to last, is Democracy,
— that it is a work conceived and carried forward in

the spirit of the genius of humanity that is now in full career in the New World, — and that all things characteristically American (trades, tools, occupations, productions, characters, scenes) therefore have their places in it. It is intended to be a complete mirror of the times in which the life of the poet fell, and to show one master personality accepting, absorbing all and rising superior to it, — namely, the poet himself. Yet it is never Whitman that speaks so much as it is Democracy that speaks through him. He personifies the spirit of universal brotherhood, and in this character launches forth his "omnivorous words." What would seem colossal egotism, shameless confessions, or unworthy affiliations with low, rude persons, what would seem confounding good and bad, virtue and vice, etc., in Whitman the man, the citizen, but serves to illustrate the boundless compassion and saving power of Whitman as the spokesman of ideal Democracy. With this clew in mind, many difficult things are made plain and easy in the works of this much misunderstood poet.

Perhaps the single poem that throws most light upon his aims and methods, and the demand he makes upon his reader, is in "Calamus," and is as follows: —

"Whoever you are holding me now in hand,
Without one thing all will be useless,
I give you fair warning before you attempt me further,
I am not what you suppos'd, but far different.

HIS RULING IDEAS AND AIMS

"Who is he that would become my follower?
Who would sign himself a candidate for my affections?

"The way is suspicious, the result uncertain, perhaps
      destructive,
You would have to give up all else, I alone would expect
      to be your sole and exclusive standard,
Your novitiate would even then be long and exhausting,
The whole past theory of your life and all conformity
      to the lives around you would have to be aban-
      don'd,
Therefore release me now before troubling yourself any
      further, let go your hand from my shoulders,
Put me down and depart on your way.

"Or else by stealth in some wood for trial,
Or back of a rock in the open air
(For in any roof'd room of a house I emerge not, nor in
      company,
And in libraries I lie as one dumb, a gawk, or unborn, or
      dead),
But just possibly with you on a high hill, first watching
      lest any person for miles around approach un-
      awares,
Or possibly with you sailing at sea, or on the beach of the
      sea or some quiet island,
Here to put your lips upon mine I permit you,
With the comrade's long-dwelling kiss or the new hus-
      band's kiss,
For I am the new husband and I am the comrade.

93

"Or, if you will, thrusting me beneath your clothing,
Where I may feel the throbs of your heart or rest upon
     your hip,
Carry me when you go forth over land or sea;
For thus merely touching you is enough, is best,
And thus touching you would I silently sleep and be car-
     ried eternally.

"But these leaves conning you con at peril,
For these leaves and me you will not understand,
They will elude you at first and still more afterward, I will
     certainly elude you,
Even while you should think you had unquestionably
     caught me, behold!
Already you see I have escaped from you.

"For it is not for what I have put into it that I have writ-
     ten this book,
Nor is it by reading it you will acquire it,
Nor do those know me best who admire me and vauntingly
     praise me,
Nor will the candidates for my love (unless at most a very
     few) prove victorious,
Nor will my poems do good only, they will do just as much
     evil, perhaps more,
For all is useless without that which you may guess at
     many times and not hit, that which I hinted at,
Therefore release me and depart on your way."

When one has fully mastered this poem he has
got a pretty good hold upon Whitman's spirit and

method. His open-air standards, the baffling and elusive character of his work, the extraordinary demand it makes, its radical and far-reaching effects upon life, its direct cognizance of evil as a necessary part of the good (there was a human need of sin, said Margaret Fuller), its unbookish spirit and affiliations, its indirect and suggestive method, that it can be fully read only through our acquaintance with life and real things at first hand, etc., — all this and more is in the poem.

28660

U10

HIS SELF–RELIANCE

IT is over sixty years since Goethe said that to be a German author was to be a German martyr. I presume things have changed in Germany since those times, and that the Goethe of to-day does not encounter the jealousy and hatred the great poet and critic of Weimar seemed to have called forth. In Walt Whitman we in America have known an American author who was an American martyr in a more literal sense than any of the men named by the great German. More than Heine, or Rousseau, or Molière, or Byron, was Whitman a victim of the literary Philistinism of his country and times; but, fortunately for himself, his was a nature so large, tolerant, and self-sufficing that his martyrdom sat very lightly upon him. His unpopularity was rather a tonic to him than otherwise. It was of a kind that tries a man's mettle, and brings out his heroic traits if he has any. One almost envies him his unpopularity. It was of the kind that only the greatest ones have experienced, and that attests something extraordinary in the recipient of it. He said he was more resolute because all had denied him than he ever could have been had all accepted, and he added: —

"I heed not and have never heeded either cautions, ma-
jorities, nor ridicule."

There are no more precious and tonic pages in
history than the records of men who have faced
unpopularity, odium, hatred, ridicule, detraction, in
obedience to an inward voice, and never lost courage
or good-nature. Whitman's is the most striking
case in our literary annals, — probably the most
striking one in our century outside of politics and
religion. The inward voice alone was the oracle he
obeyed: "My commission obeying, to question it
never daring."

The bitter-sweet cup of unpopularity he drained
to its dregs, and drained it cheerfully, as one knowing beforehand that it is preparing for him and cannot be avoided.

"Have you learn'd lessons only of those who admired you
and were tender with you? and stood aside for
you?
Have you not learn'd great lessons from those who reject
you, and brace themselves against you? or who
treat you with contempt, or dispute the passage
with you?"

Every man is a partaker in the triumph of him
who is always true to himself and makes no com-
promises with customs, schools, or opinions. Whitman's life, underneath its easy tolerance and cheerful good-will, was heroic. He fought his battle

against great odds and he conquered; he had his own way, he yielded not a hair to the enemy.

The pressure brought to bear upon him by the press, by many of his friends, and by such a man as Emerson, whom he deeply reverenced, to change or omit certain passages from his poems, seems only to have served as the opposing hammer that clinched the nail. The louder the outcry the more deeply he felt it his duty to stand by his first convictions. The fierce and scornful opposition to his sex poems, and to his methods and aims generally, was probably more confirmatory than any approval could have been. It went to the quick. During a dark period of his life, when no publisher would touch his book and when its exclusion from the mails was threatened, and poverty and paralysis were upon him, a wealthy Philadelphian offered to furnish means for its publication if he would omit certain poems ; but the poet does not seem to have been tempted for one moment by the offer. He cheerfully chose the heroic part, as he always did.

Emerson reasoned and remonstrated with him for hours, walking up and down Boston Common, and after he had finished his argument, says Whitman, which was unanswerable, " I felt down in my soul the clear and unmistakable conviction to disobey all, and pursue my own way." He told Emerson so, whereupon they went and dined together. The independence of the poet probably impressed Emerson more than his yielding would have done, for had not he preached the adamantine doctrine of self-trust? "To believe your own thought," he says, "to believe that what is true for you in your private heart is true of all men, — that is genius."

In many ways was Whitman, quite unconsciously to himself, the man Emerson invoked and prayed for, — the absolutely self-reliant man; the man who should find his own day and land sufficient; who had no desire to be Greek, or Italian, or French, or English, but only himself; who should not whine, or apologize, or go abroad; who should not duck, or deprecate, or borrow ; and who could see through the many disguises and debasements of our times the lineaments of the same gods that so ravished the bards of old.

The moment a man "acts for himself," says Emerson, "tossing the laws, the books, idolatries, and customs out of the window, we pity him no more, but thank and revere him."

Whitman took the philosopher at his word. "Greatness once and forever has done with opinion," even the opinion of the good Emerson. "Heroism works in contradiction to the voice of mankind, and in contradiction, for a time, to the voice of the great and good." "Every heroic act measures itself by its contempt of some external good," — popularity, for instance. "The characteristic of heroism is persistency." "When you have chosen your part abide by it, and do not weakly try to reconcile yourself with the world." "Adhere to your act, and congratulate yourself if you have done something strange and extravagant, and broken the monotony of a decorous age." Heroism "is the avowal of the unschooled man that he finds a quality in him that is negligent of expense, of health, of life, of danger, of hatred, of reproach, and knows that his will is higher and more excellent than all actual and all possible antagonists." "A man is to carry himself in the presence of all opposition as if everything were titular and ephemeral but he." "Great works of art," he again says, "teach us to abide by our spontaneous impression with good-natured inflexibility, the more when the whole cry of voices is on the other side."

These brave sayings of Emerson were all illustrated and confirmed by Whitman's course. The spectacle of this man sitting there by the window of his little house in Camden, poor and partially paralyzed, and looking out upon the trite and commonplace scenes and people, or looking athwart the years and seeing only detraction and denial, yet always serene, cheerful, charitable, his wisdom and tolerance ripening and mellowing with time, is something to treasure and profit by. He was a man who needed no assurances. He had the patience and the leisure of nature. He welcomed your friendly and sympathetic word, or with equal composure he did without it.

I remember calling upon him shortly after Swinburne's fierce onslaught upon him had been published, some time in the latter part of the eighties. I was curious to see how Whitman took it, but I could not discover either in word or look that he was disturbed a particle by it. He spoke as kindly of Swinburne as ever. If he was pained at all, it was on Swinburne's account and not on his own. It was a sad spectacle to see a man retreat upon himself as Swinburne had done. In fact I think hostile criticism, fiercely hostile, gave Whitman nearly as much comfort as any other. Did it not attest reality? Men do not brace themselves against shadows. Swinburne's polysyllabic rage showed the force of the current he was trying to stem. As for Swinburne's hydrocephalic muse, I do not think Whitman took any interest in it from the first.

Self-reliance, or self-trust, is one of the principles Whitman announces in his "Laws for Creations." He saw that no first-class work is possible except it issue from a man's deepest, most radical self.

"What do you suppose creation is?

What do you suppose will satisfy the soul but to walk free and own no superior?

What do you suppose I would intimate to you in a hun-

dred ways, but that man or woman is as good as
God?

And that there is no God any more divine than yourself?

And that that is what the oldest and newest myths finally
mean?

And that you or any one must approach creations through
such laws?"

I think it probable that Whitman anticipated a
long period of comparative oblivion for himself and
his works. He knew from the first that the public
would not be with him; he knew that the censors
of taste, the critics and literary professors, would
not be with him; he knew that the vast army
of Philistia, the respectable, fashionable mammon-
worshiping crowd, would not be with him, — that
the timid, the pampered, the prurient, the conforming, the bourgeoisie spirit, the class spirit, the aca-
demic spirit, the Pharisaic spirit in all its forms,
would all work against him; and that, as in the
case of nearly all original, first-class men, he would
have to wait to be understood for the growth of the
taste of himself. None knew more clearly than he
did how completely our people were under the illusion of the genteel and the conventional, and that,
even among the emancipated few, the possession of
anything like robust æsthetic perception was rare
enough. America, so bold and original and independent in the world of practical politics and material
endeavor, is, in spiritual and imaginative regions,

timid, conforming, imitative. There is, perhaps, no civilized country in the world wherein the native, original man, the real critter, as Whitman loved to say, that underlies all our culture and conventions, crops out so little in manners, in literature, and in social usages. The fear of being unconventional is greater with us than the fear of death. A certain evasiveness, polish, distrust of ourselves, amounting to insipidity and insincerity, is spoken of by observant foreigners. In other words, we are perhaps the least like children of any people in the world. All these things were against Whitman, and will continue to be against him for a long time. With the first stroke he broke through the conventional and took his stand upon the natural. With rude hands he tore away the veils and concealments from the body and from the soul. He ignored entirely all social and conventional usages and hypocrisies, not by revolt against them, but by choosing a point of view from which they disappeared. He embraced the unrefined and the savage as well as the tender and human. The illusions of the past, the models and standards, he freed himself of at once, and declared for the beauty and the divinity of the now and the here. The rude realism of his "Leaves" shocked like a plunge in the surf, but it invigorated also, if we were strong enough to stand it.

Out of Whitman's absolute self-trust arose his

prophetic egotism, — the divine fervor and audacity of the simple ego. He shared the conviction of the old prophets that man is a part of God, and that there is nothing in the universe any more divine than the individual soul. "I, too," he says, and this line is the key to much there is in his work —

"I, too, have felt the resistless call of myself."

With the old Biblical writers the motions of their own spirits, their thoughts, their dreams, were as the voice of God. There is something of the same sort in Whitman. The voice of that inner self was final and authoritative with him. It was the voice of God. He could drive through and over all the conventions of the world in obedience to that voice. This call to him was as a voice from Sinai. One of his mastering thoughts was the thought of identity, — that you are you, and I am I. This was the final meaning of things, and the meaning of immortality. "Yourself, *yourself*, YOURSELF," he says, with swelling vehemence, "forever and ever." To be compacted and riveted and fortified in yourself, so as to be a law unto yourself, is the final word of the past and of the present.

II

The shadow of Whitman's self-reliance and heroic self-esteem — the sort of eddy or back-water — was undoubtedly a childlike fondness for praise and for seeing his name in print. In his relaxed moments, when the stress of his task was not upon him, he was indeed in many respects a child. He had a child's delight in his own picture. He enjoyed hearing himself lauded as Colonel Ingersoll lauded him in his lecture in Philadelphia, and as his friends lauded him at his birthday dinner parties during the last two or three years of his life; he loved to see his name in print, and items about himself in the newspapers; he sometimes wrote them himself and gave them to the reporters. And yet nothing is surer than that he shaped his life and did his work absolutely indifferent to either praise or blame; in fact, that he deliberately did that which he knew would bring him dispraise. The candor and openness of the man's nature would not allow him to conceal or feign anything. If he loved praise, why should he not be frank about it? Did he not lay claim to the vices and vanities of men also? At its worst, Whitman's vanity was but the foible of a great nature, and should count for but little in the final estimate. The common human nature to which he lay claim will assert itself; it is not always to be kept up to the heroic pitch.

III

It was difficult to appreciate his liking for the newspaper. But he had been a newspaper man himself; the printer's ink had struck in; he had

many associations with the press-room and the com-
posing-room; he loved the common, democratic
character of the newspaper; it was the average
man's library. The homely uses to which it was
put, and the humble firesides to which it found its
way, endeared it to him, and made him love to see
his name in it.

Whitman's vanity was of the innocent, good-
natured kind. He was as tolerant of your criticism
as of your praise. Selfishness, in any unworthy
sense, he had none. Offensive arrogance and self-
assertion, in his life there was none.

His egotism is of the large generous species that
never irritates or pricks into you like that of the
merely conceited man. His love, his candor, his
sympathy are on an equal scale.

His egotism comes finally to affect one like the
independence and indifference of natural law. It
takes little heed of our opinion, whether it be for or
against, and keeps to its own way whatever befall.

Whitman's absolute faith in himself was a part
of his faith in creation. He felt himself so keenly
a part of the whole that he shared its soundness
and excellence; he must be good as it is good.

IV

Whitman showed just enough intention, or pre-
meditation in his life, dress, manners, attitudes in
his pictures, self-portrayals in his poems, etc., to give

rise to the charge that he was a *poseur*. He was a *poseur* in the sense, and to the extent, that any man is a *poseur* who tries to live up to a certain ideal and to realize it in his outward daily life. It is clear that he early formed the habit of self-contemplation and of standing apart and looking upon himself as another person. Hence his extraordinary self-knowledge, and, we may also say, his extraordinary self-appreciation, or to use his own words, "the quite changed attitude of the ego, the one chanting or talking, towards himself." Of course there is danger in this attitude, but Whitman was large enough and strong enough to escape it. He saw himself to be the typical inevitable democrat that others have seen him to be, and with perfect candor and without ever forcing the note, he portrays himself as such. As his work is confessedly the poem of himself, himself magnified and projected, as it were, upon the canvas of a great age and country, all his traits and qualities stand out in heroic proportions, his pride and egotism as well as his love and tolerance.

"How beautiful is candor," he says. "All faults may be forgiven of him who has perfect candor." The last thing that could ever be charged of Whitman is that he lacked openness, or was guilty of any deceit or concealments in his life or works.

From the studies, notes, and scrap-books which Whitman left, it appears that he was long preparing

and disciplining himself for the work he had in view.
" The long foreground," to which Emerson referred
in his letter, was of course a reality. But this self-
consciousness and self-adjustment to a given end is
an element of strength and not of weakness.

In the famous vestless and coatless portrait of
himself prefixed to the first " Leaves of Grass " he
assumes an attitude and is in a sense a *poseur* ;
but the reader comes finally to wonder at the mar-
velous self-knowledge the picture displays, and how
strictly typical it is of the poet's mental and spiritual attitude towards the world, — independent, unconventional, audacious, yet inquiring and sympathetic in a wonderful degree. In the same way he
posed in other portraits. A favorite with him is
the one in which he sits contemplating a butterfly
upon his forefinger — typical of a man " preoccupied
of his own soul." In another he peers out curiously
as from behind a mask. In an earlier one he stands,
hat in hand, in marked *negligé* costume, — a little
too intentional, one feels. The contempt of the polished ones is probably very strong within him at this
time. I say contempt, though I doubt if Whitman
ever felt contempt for any human being.

v

Then Whitman had a curious habit of standing
apart, as it were, and looking upon himself and his
career as of some other person. He was interested
in his own cause, and took a hand in the discussion.

From first to last he had the habit of regarding himself objectively. On his deathbed he seemed to be a spectator of his own last moments, and was seen to feel his pulse a few minutes before he breathed his last.

He has recorded this trait in his poems: —

"Apart from the pulling and hauling stands what I am,
Stands amused, complacent, compassionate, idle, waiting,
Looking with side-curved head curious what will come
    next,
Both in and out of the game and watching and wondering
    at it."

As also in this from " Calamus : " —

"That shadow my likeness that goes to and fro seeking a
    livelihood, chattering, chaffering,
How often I find myself standing and looking at it where
    it flits,
How often I question and doubt whether that is really me;
But among my lovers, and caroling these songs,
Oh, I never doubt whether that is really me."

Whitman always speaks as one having authority and not as a scribe, not as a mere man of letters. This is the privilege of the divine egoism of the prophet.

Like the utterances of the Biblical writers, without argument, without elaboration, his mere dictum seems the word of fate. It is not the voice of a man who has made his way through the world by rejecting and denying, but by accepting all and rising superior. What the "push of reading" or the push of argument could not start is often started and clinched by his mere authoritative "I say."

"I say where liberty draws not the blood out of slavery,
    there slavery draws the blood out of liberty, . . .

"I say the human shape or face is so great it must never be
    made ridiculous;
I say for ornaments nothing outré can be allowed,
And that anything is most beautiful without ornament,
And that exaggerations will be sternly revenged in your own
    physiology and in other persons' physiologies also.

"Think of the past;
I warn you that in a little while others will find their past
    in you and your times. . . .
Think of spiritual results.
Sure as the earth swims through the heavens, does every
    one of its objects pass into spiritual results.
Think of manhood, and you to be a man;
Do you count manhood, and the sweet of manhood, no-
    thing?
Think of womanhood and you to be a woman;
The Creation is womanhood;
Have I not said that womanhood involves all?
Have I not told how the universe has nothing better than
    the best womanhood?"

Egotism is usually intolerant, but Whitman was one of the most tolerant of men.

A craving for sympathy and personal affection he certainly had; to be valued as a human being was more to him than to be valued as a poet. His strongest attachments were probably for persons who had no opinion, good or bad, of his poetry at all.

VI

Under close scrutiny his egotism turns out to be a kind of altru-egotism, which is vicarious and all-inclusive of his fellows. It is one phase of his democracy, and is vital and radical in his pages. It is a high, imperturbable pride in his manhood and in the humanity which he shares with all. It is the exultant and sometimes almost arrogant expression of the feeling which underlies and is shaping the whole modern world — the feeling and conviction that the individual man is above all forms, laws, institutions, conventions, bibles, religions — that the divinity of kings, and the sacredness of priests of the old order, pertains to the humblest person.

It was a passion that united him to his fellows rather than separated him from them. His pride was not that of a man who sets himself up above others, or who claims some special advantage or privilege, but that godlike quality that would make others share its great good-fortune. Hence we are not at all shocked when the poet, in the fervor of his love for mankind, determinedly imputes to himself all the sins and vices and follies of his fellow-men. We rather glory in it. This self-abasement is the seal of the authenticity of his egotism. Without those things there might be some ground for the complaint of a Boston critic of Whitman that his work was not noble, because it celebrated pride, and did not inculcate the virtues of humility and self-denial. The great lesson of the " Leaves," flowing curiously out of its pride and egotism, is the lesson of charity, of self-surrender, and the free bestowal of yourself upon all hands.

The law of life of great art is the law of life in ethics, and was long ago announced.

He that would lose his life shall find it; he who gives himself the most freely shall the most freely receive. Whitman made himself the brother and equal of all, not in word, but in very deed; he was in himself a compend of the people for which he spoke, and this breadth of sympathy and free giving of himself has resulted in an unexpected accession of power.

HIS RELATION TO ART AND LITERATURE

I

WHITMAN protests against his "Leaves" being judged merely as literature; but at the same time, if they are not good literature, that of course ends the matter. Still, while the questions of art, of form, of taste, are paramount in most other poets, — certainly in all third and fourth rate poets, — in Whitman they are swallowed up in other questions and values.

In numerous passages, by various figures and allegories, Whitman indicates that he would not have his book classed with the order of mere literary productions.

"Shut not your doors to me, proud libraries," he says in one of the "Inscriptions," —

"For that which was lacking in all your well-fill'd shelves,
    yet needed most, I bring.
Forth from the war emerging, a book I have made,
The words of my book nothing, the drift of it everything,
A book separate, not link'd with the rest nor felt by the
    intellect,
But you, ye untold latencies will thrill to every page."

Not linked with the studied and scholarly productions, not open to the mere bookish mind, but more akin to the primitive utterances and oracles of historic humanity. A literary age like ours lays great stress upon the savor of books, art, culture, and has little taste for the savor of real things, the real man, which we get in Whitman.

"It is the true breath of humanity," says Renan, "and not literary merit, that constitutes the beautiful." An Homeric poem written to-day, he goes on to say, would not be beautiful, because it would not be true; it would not contain this breath of a living humanity. "It is not Homer who is beautiful, it is the Homeric life." The literary spirit begat Tennyson, begat Browning, begat New England poets, but it did not in the same sense beget Whitman, any more than it begat Homer or Job or Isaiah. The artist may delight in him and find his own ideals there; the critic may study him and find the poet master of all his weapons; the disciple of culture will find, as Professor Triggs has well said, that "there is no body of writings in literature which demands a wider conversancy with the best that has been thought or said in the world," — yet the poet escapes from all hands that would finally hold him and monopolize him. Whitman is an immense solvent, — forms, theories, rules, criticisms, disappear in his fluid, teeming pages. Much can be deduced from him, because much went

to the making up of his point of view. He makes
no criticism, yet a far-reaching criticism is implied in the very start of his poems. No modern
poet presupposes so much, or requires so much
preliminary study and reflection. He brings a
multitude of questions and problems, and, what
is singular, he brings them in himself; they are
implied in his temper, and in his attitude toward
life and reality.

Whitman says he has read his "Leaves" to himself in the open air, that he has tried himself by
the elemental laws; and tells us in many ways,
direct and indirect, that the standards he would be
tried by are not those of art or books, but of absolute nature. He has been laughed at for calling
himself a "Kosmos," but evidently he uses the
term to indicate this elemental, dynamic character
of his work, — its escape from indoor, artificial
standards, its aspiration after the "amplitude of
the earth, and the coarseness and sexuality of the
earth, and the great charity of the earth, and the
equilibrium also."

II

Unless the poetic perception is fundamental in
us, and can grasp the poetry of things, actions,
characters, multitudes, heroisms, we shall read
Whitman with very poor results. Unless America,
the contemporary age, life, nature, are poetical to

117

us, Whitman will not be. He has aimed at the larger poetry of forces, masses, persons, enthusiasms, rather than at the poetry of the specially rare and fine. He kindles in me the delight I have in space, freedom, power, the elements, the cosmic, democracy, and the great personal qualities of self-reliance, courage, candor, charity.

Always in the literary poets are we impressed with the art of the poet as something distinct from the poet himself, and more or less put on. The poet gets himself up for the occasion; he assumes the pose and the language of the poet, as the priest assumes the pose and the language of devotion. In Whitman the artist and the man are one. He never gets himself up for the occasion. Our pleasure in him is rarely or never our pleasure in the well-dressed, the well-drilled, the cultivated, the refined, the orderly, but it is more akin to our pleasure in real things, in human qualities and powers, in freedom, health, development. Yet I never open his book without being struck afresh with its pictural quality, its grasp of the concrete, its vivid realism, its intimate sense of things, persons, truths, qualities, such as only the greatest artists can give us, and such as we can never get in mere prose. It is as direct as a challenge, as personal as a handshake, and yet withal how mystical, how elusive, how incommensurable! To deny that Whitman belongs to the fraternity of great artists, the shapers and moulders of the ideal, — those who breathe the breath of life into the clay or stone of common facts and objects, who make all things plastic and the vehicles of great and human emotions, — is to read him very inadequately, to say the least. To get at Walt Whitman you must see through just as much as you do in dealing with nature; you are to bring the same interpretive imagination. You are not to be balked by what appears to be the coarse and the familiar, or by his rank contemporaneity; after a time you will surely see the lambent spiritual flames that play about it all, —

"Prophetic spirit of materials shifting and flickering
    about me," —

and his cosmic splendor, depth, and power. It is not the denial of art, it is a new affirmation of life. It is one phase of his democracy. It is the logical conclusion of the vestless and coatless portrait of himself that appeared in the first edition of his poems. He would give us more of the man, a fuller measure of personal, concrete, human qualities than any poet before him. He strips away the artificial wrappings and illusions usual in poetry, and relies entirely upon the native and intrinsic. He will have no curtains, he says, — not the finest, — between himself and his reader.

"Stop this day and night with me and you shall possess
    the origin of all poems,

You shall possess the good of the earth and sun (there are
    millions of suns left),
You shall no longer take things at second or third hand,
    nor look through the eyes of the dead, nor feed on
    the spectres in books,
You shall not look through my eyes either, nor take things
    from me,
You shall listen to all sides and filter them from your-
    self."

This is a hint of his democracy as applied to
literature, — more direct and immediate contact
with the primary and universal, less of the vestments
and trappings of art and more of the push and power
of original character and of nature.

III

It seems to me it is always in order to protest
against the narrow and dogmatic spirit that so often
crops out in current criticism touching this matter
of art. "The boundaries of art are jealously
guarded," says a recent authority, as if art had
boundaries like a state or province that had been
accurately surveyed and fixed, — as if art was a fact
and not a spirit.

Now I shall deny at the outset that there are
any bounds of art, or that art is in any sense an
"enclosure," — a province fenced off and set apart
from the rest, — any more than religion is an enclosure, though so many people would like to make it

120

so. Art is commensurate with the human spirit. I should even deny that there are any principles of art in the sense that there are principles of mechanics or of mathematics. Art has but one principle, one aim, — to produce an impression, a powerful impression, no matter by what means, or if it be by reversing all the canons of taste and criticism. Name any principle, so called, and some day a genius shall be born who will produce his effects in defiance of it, or by appearing to reverse it. Such a man as Turner seemed, at first sight, to set at defiance all correct notions of art. The same with Wagner in music, the same with Whitman in poetry. The new man is impossible till he appears, and, when he appears, in proportion to his originality and power does it take the world a longer or shorter time to adjust its critical standards to him. But it is sure to do so at last. There is nothing final in art: its principles follow and do not lead the creator; they are deductions from his work, not its inspiration. We demand of the new man, of the overthrower of our idols, but one thing, — has he authentic inspiration and power? If he has not, his pretensions are soon exploded. If he has, we cannot put him down, any more than we can put down a law of nature, and we very soon find some principle of art that fits his case. Is there no room for the new man? But the new man makes room for himself, and if he be of the first order he largely makes the taste by which he is appreciated, and the rules of art by which he is to be judged.

IV

The trouble with most of us is that we found our taste for poetry upon particular authors, instead of upon literature as a whole, or, better yet, upon life and reality. Hence we form standards instead of principles. Standards are limited, rigid, uncompromising, while principles are flexible, expansive, creative. If we are wedded to the Miltonic standard of poetry, the classic standards, we shall have great difficulties with Whitman; but if we have founded our taste upon natural principles — if we have learned to approach literature through reality, instead of reality through literature — we shall not be the victims of any one style or model; we shall be made free of all. The real test of art, of any art, as Burke long ago said, and as quoted by Mr. Howells in his trenchant little volume called " Criticism and Fiction," is to be sought outside of art, namely, in nature. " I can judge but poorly of anything while I measure it by no other standard than itself. The true standard of the arts is in every man's power; and an easy observation of the most common, sometimes of the meanest, things in nature will give the truest lights." It is thought that the preëminence of the Greek standards is settled when we say they are natural. Yes, but Nature is not Greek. She is Asiatic, German, English, as well.

v

In poetry, in art, a man must sustain a certain vital relation to his work, and that work must sustain a certain vital relation to the laws of mind and of life. That is all, and that leaves the doors very wide. We are not to ask, Is it like this or like that? but, Is it vital, is it real, is it a consistent, well-organized whole?

The poet must always interpret himself and nature after his own fashion. Is his fashion adequate? Is the interpretation vivid and real? Do his lines cut to the quick, and beget heat and joy in the soul? If we cannot make the poet's ideal our own by sharing his enthusiasm for it, the trouble is as likely to be in ourselves as in him. In any case he must be a law unto himself.

The creative artist differs from the mere writer or thinker in this: he sustains a direct personal relation to his subject through emotion, intuition, will. The indirect, impersonal relation which works by reflection, comparison, and analysis is that of the critic and philosopher. The man is an artist when he gives us a concrete and immediate impression of reality: from his hands we get the thing itself; from the critic and thinker we get ideas *about* the thing. The poet does not merely say the world is beautiful; he shows it as beautiful: he does not

123

describe the flower; he places it before us. What are the enemies of art? Reflection, didacticism, description, the turgid, the obscure. A poet with a thesis to sustain is more or less barred from the freedom of pure art. It is by direct and unconsidered expression, says Scherer, that art communicates with reality. The things that make for art, then, are feeling, intuition, sentiment, soul, a fresh and vigorous sense of real things, — in fact, all that makes for life, health, and wholeness. Goethe is more truly an artist in the first part of Faust than in the second; Arnold has a more truly artistic mind than Lowell.

The principles of art are always the same in the respect I have indicated, just as the principles of life are always the same, or of health and longevity are always the same. No writer is an artist who is related to his subject simply by mental or logical grip alone: he must have a certain emotional affiliation and identity with it; he does not so much convey to us ideas and principles as pictures, parables, impressions, — a lively sense of real things. When we put Whitman outside the pale of art, we must show his shortcomings here; we must show that he is not fluid and generative, — that he paints instead of interprets, that he gives us reasons instead of impulses, a stone when we ask for bread. "I do not give a little charity," he says; "when I give, I give myself." This the artist always does,

124

not his mind merely, but his soul, his personality. "Leaves of Grass" is as direct an emanation from a central personal force as any book in literature, and always carries its own test and its own proof. It never hardens into a system, it never ceases to be penetrated with will and emotion, it never declines from the order of deeds to the order of mere thoughts. All is movement, progress, evolution, picture, parable, impulse.

It is on these grounds that Whitman, first of all, is an artist. He has the artist temperament. His whole life was that of a man who lives to ideal ends, — who lives to bestow himself upon others, to extract from life its meaning and its joy.

VI

Whitman has let himself go, and trusted himself to the informal and spontaneous, to a degree unprecedented. His course required a self-reliance of the highest order; it required an innate cohesion and homogeneity, a firmness and consistency of individual outline, that few men have. It would seem to be much easier to face the poet's problem in the old, well-worn forms — forms that are so winsome and authoritative in themselves — than to stand upon a basis so individual and intrinsic as Whitman chose to stand upon. His course goes to the quick at once. How much of a man are you? How vital and fundamental is your

125

poetic gift ? Can it go alone ? Can it face us in undress ?

Never did the artist more cunningly conceal himself; never did he so completely lose himself in the man, identifying himself with the natural and spontaneous; never emerging and challenging attention on his own account, denying us when we too literally seek him, mocking us when we demand his credentials, and revealing himself only when we have come to him upon his own terms.

The form the poet chose favored this self-revelation; there is nothing, no outside conscious art, to stand between himself and his reader. "This is no book," he says: "who touches this touches a man." In one sense Whitman is without art, — the impression which he always seeks to make is that of reality itself. He aims to give us reality without the usual literary veils and illusions, — the least possible amount of the artificial, the extrinsic, the put-on, between himself and his reader. He banishes from his work, as far as possible, what others are so intent upon, — all atmosphere of books and culture, all air of literary intention and decoration, — and puts his spirit frankly and immediately to his readers. The verse does not seem to have been shaped; it might have grown: it takes no apparent heed of externals, but flows on like a brook, irregular, rhythmical, and always fluid and real. A cry will always be raised against the producer in any field who discards the authority of the models and falls back upon simple Nature, or upon himself, as Millet did in painting, and Wagner in music, and Whitman in poetry.

Whitman's working ideas, the principles that inspired him, are all directly related to life and the problems of life; they are democracy, nature, freedom, love, personality, religion: while the ideas from which our poets in the main draw their inspiration are related to art, — they are literary ideas, such as lucidity, form, beauty.

VII

Much light is thrown upon Whitman's literary methods and aims by a remark which he once made in conversation with Dr. Bucke: —

"I have aimed to make the book simple, — tasteless, or with little taste, — with very little or no perfume. The usual way is for the poet or writer to put in as much taste, perfume, piquancy, as he can; but this is not the way of nature, which I take for model. Nature presents us her productions — her air, earth, waters, even her flowers, grains, meats — with faint and delicate flavor and fragrance, but these in the long run make the deepest impression. Man, dealing with natural things, constantly aims to increase their piquancy. By crossing and selection he deepens and intensifies the scents and hues of flowers, the tastes of fruits, and so on. He pur-

127

sues the same method in poetry, — that is, strives for strong light or shade, for high color, perfume, pungency, in all ways for the greatest immediate effect. In so doing he leaves the true way, the way of Nature, and, in the long run, comes far short of producing her effects."

More light of the same kind is thrown upon his methods by the following passage from the preface to the first edition of his poems in 1855.

"To speak in literature," he says, "with the perfect rectitude and insouciance of the movements of animals, and the unimpeachableness of the sentiment of trees in the woods and grass by the roadside, is the flawless triumph of art." And again: "The great poet has less a marked style, and is more the channel of thoughts and things without increase or diminution, and is the free channel of himself. He swears to his art, I will not be meddlesome; I will not have in my writing any elegance, or effect, or originality, to hang in the way between me and the rest like curtains. I will have nothing hang in the way, not the richest curtains. What I tell, I tell for precisely what it is. Let who may exalt or startle or fascinate or soothe, I will have purpose, as health or heat or snow has, and be as regardless of observation. What I experience or portray shall go from my composition without a shred of my composition. You shall stand by my side and look in the mirror with me."

VIII

But in view of the profound impression Whitman's work has made upon widely different types of mind on both sides of the Atlantic, and in view of the persistent vitality of his fame, the question whether he is inside or outside the pale of art amounts to very little. I quite agree with the late Mrs. Gilchrist, that, when "great meanings and great emotions are expressed with corresponding power, literature has done its best, call it what you please."

That Whitman has expressed great meanings and great emotions with adequate power, even his unfriendly critics admit. Thus Professor Wendell, in an admirable essay on American literature, says that "though Whitman is uncouth, inarticulate, and lacking in a grotesque degree artistic form, yet for all that he can make you feel for the moment how even the ferry-boats plying from New York to Brooklyn are fragments of God's eternities." In the same way Mr. William Clark, his British critic and expounder, says that he is wanting in discrimination and art, "flings his ideas at us in a heap," etc., and yet that the effect of his work is "to stir our emotions, widen our interests, and rally the forces of our moral nature."

It seems to me that a man who, through the printed page, can do these things, must have some kind of art worth considering. If, through his impassioned treatment of a prosy, commonplace object like a ferry-boat, he can so dignify and exalt it, and so fill it with the meanings of the spirit, that it seems like a part of God's eternities, his methods are at least worth inquiring into.

The truth is, Whitman's art, in its lack of extrinsic form and finish, is Oriental rather than Occidental, and is an offense to a taste founded upon the precision and finish of a mechanical age. His verse is like the irregular, slightly rude coin of the Greeks compared with the exact, machine-cut dies of our own day, or like the unfinished look of Japanese pottery beside the less beautiful but more perfect specimens of modern ceramic art.

For present purposes, we may say there are two phases of art, — formal art and creative art. By formal art I mean that which makes a direct appeal to our sense of form, — our sense of the finely carved, the highly wrought, the deftly planned; and by creative art I mean that quickening, fructifying power of the masters, that heat and passion that make the world plastic and submissive to their hands, teeming with new meanings and thrilling with new life.

Formal art is always in the ascendant. Formal anything — formal dress, formal manners, formal religion, formal this and that — always counts for more than the informal, the spontaneous, the original. It is easier, it can be put off and on.

Formal art is nearly always the gift of the minor poet, and often of the major poet also. In such a poet as Swinburne, formal art leads by a great way. The content of his verse, — what is it? In Tennyson as well I should say formal art is in the ascendant. Creative art is his also; Tennyson reaches and moves the spirit, yet his skill is more noteworthy than his power. In Wordsworth, on the other hand, I should say creative art led: the content of his verse is more than its form; his spiritual and religious values are greater than his literary and artistic. The same is true of our own Emerson. Poe, again, is much more as an artist than as a man or a personality.

I hardly need say that in Whitman formal art, the ostensibly artistic, counts for but very little. The intentional artist, the professional poet, is kept entirely in abeyance, or is completely merged and hidden in the man, more so undoubtedly than in any poet this side the old Oriental bards. We call him formless, chaotic, amorphous, etc., because he makes no appeal to our modern highly stimulated sense of art or artificial form. We must discriminate this from our sense of power, our sense of life, our sense of beauty, of the sublime, of the all, which clearly Whitman would reach and move. Whitman certainly has a form of his own: what would a poet, or any writer or worker in the ideal, do without some kind of form? some consistent and adequate vehicle of expression? But Whitman's form is not what is called artistic, because it is not brought within the rules of the prosodical system, and does not appeal to our sense of the consciously shaped and cultivated. It is essentially the prose form heightened and intensified by a deep, strong, lyric, and prophetic note.

The bonds and shackles of regular verse-form Whitman threw off. This course seemed to be demanded by the spirit to which he had dedicated himself, — the spirit of absolute unconstraint. The restrictions and hamperings of the scholastic forms did not seem to be consistent with this spirit, which he identified with democracy and the New World. A poet who sets out to let down the bars everywhere, to remove veils and obstructions, to emulate the freedom of the elemental forces, to effuse always the atmosphere of open-air growths and objects, to be as "regardless of observation" as the processes of nature, will not be apt to take kindly to any arbitrary and artificial form of expression. The essentially prose form which Whitman chose is far more in keeping with the spirit and aim of his work than any conventional metrical system could have been. Had he wrought solely as a conscious artist, aiming at the effect of finely chiseled forms, he would doubtless have chosen a different medium.

132

IX

Whitman threw himself with love and enthusiasm upon this great, crude, seething, materialistic American world. The question is, Did he master it? Is he adequate to absorb and digest it? Does he make man-stuff of it? Is it plastic in his hands? Does he stamp it with his own image? I do not ask, Does he work it up into what are called artistic forms? Does he make it the quarry from which he carves statues or builds temples? because evidently he does not do this, or assume to do it. He is content if he presents America and the modern to us as they are inwrought into his own personality, bone of his bone and flesh of his flesh, or as character, passion, will, motive, conviction. He would show them subjectively and as living impulses in himself. Of course a great constructive, dramatic poet like Shakespeare would have solved his problem in a different manner, or through the objective, artistic portrayal of types and characters. But the poet and prophet of democracy and of egotism shows us all things in and through himself.

His egotism, or egocentric method, is the fundamental fact about his work. It colors all and determines all. The poems are the direct outgrowth of the personality of the poet; they are born directly upon the ego, as it were, like the fruit of that tropical tree which grows immediately upon the trunk. His work is nearer his radical, primary self than that of most poets. He never leads us away from himself into pleasant paths with enticing flowers of fancy or forms of art. He carves or shapes nothing for its own sake; there is little in the work that can stand on independent grounds as pure art. His work is not material made precious by elaboration and finish, but by its relation to himself and to the sources of life.

X

Whitman was compelled to this negation of extrinsic art by the problem he had set before himself, — first, to arouse, to suggest, rather than to finish or elaborate, less to display any theme or thought than "to bring the reader into the atmosphere of the theme or thought;" secondly, to make his own personality the chief factor in the volume, or present it so that the dominant impression should always be that of the living, breathing man as we meet him and see him and feel him in life, and never as we see him and feel him in books or art, — the man in the form and garb of actual, concrete life, not as poet or artist, but simply as man. This is doubtless the meaning of the vestless and coatless portrait of himself prefixed to the first issue of the "Leaves," to which I have referred. This portrait is symbolical of the whole attitude of the poet toward his task. It was a hint that we must take this poet with

134

very little literary tailoring; it was a hint that he belonged to the open air, and came of the people and spoke in their spirit.

It is never the theme treated, but always the character exploited; never the structure finished, but always the plan suggested; never the work accomplished, but always the impulse imparted, — freedom, power, growth.

"Allons ! we must not stop here.
However sweet these laid-up stores, however convenient
       this dwelling, we cannot remain here,
However sheltered this port, or however calm these waters,
       we must not anchor here,
However welcome the hospitality that surrounds us we are
       permitted to receive it but a little while.

"Allons! With power, liberty, the earth, the elements!
Health, defiance, gayety, self-esteem, curiosity;
Allons! from all formulas!
From your formulas, O bat-eyed and materialistic priests!"

This magnificent poem, "The Song of the Open Road," is one of the most significant in Whitman's work. He takes the open road as his type, — not an end in itself, not a fulfillment, but a start, a journey, a progression. It teaches him the profound lesson of reception, "no preference nor denial," and the profounder lesson of liberty and truth : —

135

WHITMAN

"From this hour, freedom!
From this hour I ordain myself loosed of limits and im-
aginary lines,
Going where I list — my own master, total and absolute,
Listening to others, and considering well what they say,
Pausing, searching, receiving, contemplating,
Gently, but with undeniable will, divesting myself of the
holds that would hold me.

"I inhale great draughts of air,
The east and the west are mine, and the north and the
south are mine."

He will not rest with art, he will not rest with
books, he will press his way steadily toward the
largest freedom.

"Only the kernel of every object nourishes.
Where is he who tears off the husks for you and me?
Where is he who undoes stratagems and envelopes for
you and me?"

Whitman was not a builder. If he had the archi-
tectural power which the great poets have shown,
he gave little proof of it. It was not required by the
task he set before himself. His book is not a tem-
ple: it is a wood, a field, a highway; vista, vista, everywhere, — vanishing lights and shades, truths half
disclosed, successions of objects, hints, suggestions,
brief pictures, groups, voices, contrasts, blendings,
and, above all, the tonic quality of the open air.

The shorter poems are like bunches of herbs or leaves, or a handful of sprays gathered in a walk; never a thought carefully carved, and appealing to our sense of artistic form.

The main poem of the book, "The Song of Myself," is a series of utterances, ejaculations, apostrophes, enumerations, associations, pictures, parables, incidents, suggestions, with little or no structural or logical connection, but all emanating from a personality whose presence dominates the page, and whose eye is ever upon us. Without this vivid and intimate sense of the man back of all, of a sane and powerful spirit sustaining ours, the piece would be wild and inchoate.

XI

The reader will be sure to demand of Whitman ample compensation for the absence from his work of those things which current poets give us in such full measure. Whether or not the compensation is ample, whether the music of his verse as of winds and waves, the long, irregular dithyrambic movement, its fluid and tonic character, the vastness of conception, the large, biblical speech, the surging cosmic emotion, the vivid personal presence as of the living man looking into your eye or walking by your side, — whether all these things, the refreshing quality as of "harsh salt spray" which the poet Lanier found in the "Leaves," the electric currents which Mrs. Gilchrist found there, the "un-excelled imaginative justice of language" which Mr. Stevenson at times found, the religious liberation and faith which Mr. Symonds found, the "incomparable things incomparably well said" of Emerson, the rifle bullets of Ruskin, the "supreme words" of Colonel Ingersoll, etc., — whether qualities and effects like these, I say, make up to us for the absence of the traditional poetic graces and adornments is a question which will undoubtedly long divide the reading world.

In the works upon which our poetic taste is founded, artistic form is paramount; we have never been led to apply to such works open-air standards, — clouds, trees, rivers, spaces, — but the precision and definiteness of the cultured and the artificial. If Whitman had aimed at pure art and had failed, his work would be intolerable. As his French critic, Gabriel Sarrazin, has well said: "In the large work which Whitman attempted, there come no rules save those of nobility and strength of spirit; and these suffice amply to create a most unlooked-for and grandiose aspect of beauty." "Overcrowded and disorderly" as it may seem, "if heroic emotion and thought and enthusiasm vitalize it," the poet has reached his goal.

XII

Sometimes I define Whitman to myself as the poet of the open air, — not because he sings the praises of these things after the manner of the so-called nature-poets, but because he has the quality of things in the open air, the quality of the unhoused, the untamed, the elemental and aboriginal. He pleases and he offends, the same way things at large do. He has the brawn, the indifference, the rudeness, the virility, the coarseness, — something gray, unpronounced, elemental, about him, the effect of mass, size, distance, flowing, vanishing lines, neutral spaces, — something informal, multitudinous, and processional, — something regardless of criticism, that makes no bid for our applause, not calculated instantly to please, unmindful of details, prosaic if we make it so, common, near at hand, and yet that provokes thought and stirs our emotions in an unusual degree. The long lists and catalogues of objects and scenes in Whitman, that have so excited the mirth of the critics, are one phase of his out-of-doors character, — a multitude of concrete objects, a grove, a thicket, a field, a stretch of beach, — every object sharply defined, but no attempt at logical or artistic sequence, the effect of the whole informal, multitudinous. It may be objected to these pages that they consist of a mass of details that do not make a picture. But every line is a picture of a scene or an object. Whitman always keeps up the movement, he never pauses to describe; it is all action.

Passing from such a poet as Tennyson to Whitman is like going from a warm, perfumed interior, with rich hangings, pictures, books, statuary, fine men and women, out into the street, or upon the beach, or upon the hill, or under the midnight stars. We lose something certainly, but do we not gain something also? Do we not gain just what Whitman had in view, namely, direct contact with the elements in which are the sources of our life and health? Do we not gain in scope and power what we lose in art and refinement?

The title, "Leaves of Grass," is full of meaning. What self-knowledge and self-scrutiny it implies! The grass, perennially sprouting, universal, formless, common, the always spread feast of the herds, dotted with flowers, the herbage of the earth, so suggestive of the multitudinous, loosely aggregated, unelaborated character of the book; the lines springing directly out of the personality of the poet, the soil of his life.

"What is commonest, cheapest, nearest, easiest is me,"

says the poet, and this turns out to be the case. We only look to see if in the common and the cheap he discloses new values and new meanings, — if his leaves of grass have the old freshness and nutriment, and be not a mere painted greenness.

"The pure contralto sings in the organ loft,
The carpenter dresses his plank — the tongue of his foreplane whistles its wild ascending lisp,

The married and unmarried children ride home to
     their Thanksgiving dinner,

The pilot seizes the king-pin — he heaves down with a
     strong arm,

The mate stands braced in the whale-boat — lance and
     harpoon are ready,

The duck-shooter walks by silent and cautious stretches,

The deacons are ordained with crossed hands at the altar,

The spinning-girl retreats and advances to the hum of the
     big wheel,

The farmer stops by the bars, as he walks on a First Day
     loafe, and looks at the oats and rye,

The lunatic is carried at last to the asylum, a confirmed
     case,

He will never sleep any more as he did in the cot in his
     mother's bedroom;

The jour printer with gray head and gaunt jaws works at
     his case,

He turns his quid of tobacco, while his eyes blurr with the
     manuscript;

The malformed limbs are tied to the anatomist's table,

What is removed drops horribly in a pail;

The quadroon girl is sold at the stand — the drunkard
     nods by the bar-room stove,

The machinist rolls up his sleeves — the policeman
     travels his beat — the gate-keeper marks who pass,

The young fellow drives the express-wagon — I love him,
     though I do not know him,

The half-breed straps on his light boots to compete in the
     race,

The western turkey-shooting draws old and young —
some lean on their rifles, some sit on logs,

Out from the crowd steps the marksman, takes his position, levels his piece;

The groups of newly-come emigrants cover the wharf or
levee,

As the woolly-pates hoe in the sugar-field, the overseer
views them from his saddle,

The bugle calls in the ball-room, the gentlemen run
for their partners, the dancers bow to each
other,

The youth lies awake in the cedar-roofed garret, and harks
to the musical rain,

The Wolverine sets traps on the creek that helps fill the
Huron,

The reformer ascends the platform, he spouts with his
mouth and nose,

. . . .

Seasons pursuing each other, the plougher ploughs, the
mower mows, and the winter-grain falls in the
ground,

Off on the lakes the pike-fisher watches and waits by the
hole in the frozen surface,

The stumps stand thick round the clearing, the squatter
strikes deep with his axe,

Flatboatmen make fast, towards dusk, near the cotton-
wood or pekan-trees,

Coon-seekers go through the regions of the Red River, or
through those drained by the Tennessee, or through
those of the Arkansas,

Torches shine in the dark that hangs on the Chattahooche
    or Altamahaw,
Patriarchs sit at supper with sons and grandsons and great-
    grandsons around them,
In walls of adobe, in canvas tents, rest hunters and trap-
    pers after their day's sport,
The city sleeps and the country sleeps,
The living sleep for their time, the dead sleep for their
    time,
The old husband sleeps by his wife, and the young hus-
    band sleeps by his wife;
And these one and all tend inward to me, and I tend out-
    ward to them,
And such as it is to be of these, more or less, I am."

What is this but tufts and tussocks of grass;
not branching trees, nor yet something framed
and deftly put together, but a succession of simple
things, objects, actions, persons; handfuls of native
growths, a stretch of prairie or savanna; no composition, no artistic wholes, no logical sequence, yet all
vital and real; jets of warm life that shoot and play
over the surface of contemporary America, and that
the poet uses as the stuff out of which to weave the
song of himself.

This simple aggregating or cataloguing style as
it has been called, and which often occurs in the
"Leaves," has been much criticised, but it seems to
me in perfect keeping in a work that does not aim
at total artistic effects, at finished structural perfec-

tion like architecture, but to picture the elements
of a man's life and character in outward scenes and
objects and to show how all nature tends inward to
him and he outward to it. Whitman showers the
elements of American life upon his reader until, so
to speak, his mind is drenched with them, but never
groups them into patterns to tickle his sense of
form. It is charged that his method is inartistic,
and it is so in a sense, but it is the Whitman art
and has its own value in his work. Only the artist
instinct could prompt to this succession of one line
genre word painting.

But this is not the way of the great artists. No,
but it is Whitman's way, and these things have a
certain artistic value in his work, a work that pro-
fessedly aims to typify his country and times, — the
value of multitude, processions, mass-movements,
and the gathering together of elements and forces
from wide areas.

XIII

Whitman's relation to art, then, is primary and
fundamental, just as his relations to religion, to
culture, to politics, to democracy, are primary and
fundamental, — through his emotion, his soul, and
not merely through his tools, his intellect. His
artistic conscience is quickly revealed to any searching inquiry. It is seen in his purpose to convey
his message by suggestion and indirection, or as

an informing, vitalizing breath and spirit. His
thought and meaning are enveloped in his crowded,
concrete, and often turbulent pages, as science is
enveloped in nature. He has a profound ethic,
a profound metaphysic, but they are not formulated; they are vital in his pages as hearing or
eyesight.

Whitman studied effects, and shaped his means
to his end, weighing values and subordinating parts,
as only the great artist does. He knew the power
of words as few know them; he knew the value of
vista, perspective, vanishing lights and lines. He
knew how to make his words itch at your ears till
you understood them; how to fold up and put away
in his sentences meanings, glimpses, that did not
at first reveal themselves. It is only the work of
the great creative artist that is pervaded by will,
and that emanates directly and inevitably from the
personality of the man himself. As a man and an
American, Whitman is as closely related to his
work as Æschylus to his, or Dante to his. This is
always a supreme test, — the closeness and vitality
of the relation of a man to his work. Could any
one else have done it? Is it the general intelligence
that speaks, the culture and refinement of the age?
or have we a new revelation of life, a new mind
and soul? The lesser poets sustain only a secondary
relation to their works. It is other poets, other
experiences, the past, the schools, the forms, that

speak through them. In all Whitman's recitatives, as he calls them, the free-flowing ends of the sentences, the loose threads of meaning, the unraveled or unknitted threads and fringes, are all well considered, and are one phase of *his* art. He seeks his effects thus.

His method is indirect, allegorical, and elliptical to an unusual degree; often a curious suspension and withholding in a statement, a suggestive incompleteness, both ends of his thought, as it were, left in the air; sometimes the substantive, sometimes the nominative, is wanting, and all for a purpose. The poet somewhere speaks of his utterance as "prophetic screams." The prophetic element is rarely absent, the voice of one crying in the wilderness, only it is a more jocund and reassuring cry than we are used to in prophecy. The forthrightness of utterance, the projectile force of expression, the constant appeal to unseen laws and powers of the great prophetic souls, is here.

Whitman is poetic in the same way in which he is democratic, in the same way in which he is religious, or American, or modern, — not by word merely, but by deed; not by the extrinsic, but by the intrinsic; not by art, but by life.

I am never tired of saying that to put great personal qualities in a poem, or other literary work, not formulated or didactically stated, but in tone, manner, attitude, breadth of view, love, charity, good

146

fellowship, etc., is the great triumph for our day. So put, they are a possession to the race forever; they grow and bear fruit perennially, like the grass and the trees. And shall it be said that the poet who does this has no worthy art?

XIV

Nearly all modern artificial products, when compared with the ancient, are characterized by greater mechanical finish and precision. Can we say, therefore, they are more artistic? Is a gold coin of the time of Pericles, so rude and simple, less artistic than the elaborate coins of our own day? Is Japanese pottery, the glazing often ragged and uneven, less artistic than the highly finished work of the moderns?

Are we quite sure, after all, that what we call "artistic form" is in any high or fundamental sense artistic? Are the precise, the regular, the measured, the finished, the symmetrical, indispensable to our conception of art? If regular extrinsic form and measure and proportion are necessary elements of the artistic, then geometrical flower-beds, and trees set in rows or trained to some fancy pattern, ought to please the artist. But do they? If we look for the artistic in these things, then Addison is a greater artist than Shakespeare. Dr. Johnson says, "Addison speaks the language of poets, and Shakespeare of men." Which is really the most artistic?

The one is the coin from the die, the other the coin from the hand.

Tennyson's faultless form and finish are not what stamp him a great artist. He would no doubt be glad to get rid of them if he could, at least to keep them in abeyance and make them less obtrusive; he would give anything for the freedom, raciness, and wildness of Shakespeare. But he is not equal to these things. The culture, the refinement, the precision of a correct and mechanical age have sunk too deeply into his soul. He has not the courage or the spring to let himself go as Shakespeare did. Tennyson, too, speaks the language of poets, and not of men; he savors of the flower-garden, and not of the forest. Tennyson knows that he is an artist. Shakespeare, apparently, never had such a thought; he is intent solely upon holding the mirror up to nature. Tennyson lived in an age of criticism, and when the poets loved poetry more than they did life and things; Shakespeare, in a more virile time, and in " the full stream of the world."

" Leaves of Grass " is not self-advertised as a work of art. The author had no thought that you should lay down his book and say, " What a great artist!" " What a master workman!" He would rather you should say, "What a great man!" " What a loving comrade!" " What a real democrat!" " What a healing and helpful force!" He would not have you admire his poetry: he would have you

148

filled with the breath of a new and larger and saner life; he would be a teacher and trainer of men.

The love of the precise, the exact, the methodical, is characteristic of an age of machinery, of a commercial and industrial age like ours. These things are indispensable in the mill and counting-house, but why should we insist upon them in poetry? Why should we cling to an arbitrary form like the sonnet? Why should we insist upon a perfect rhyme, as if it was a cog in a wheel? Why not allow and even welcome the freedom of half-rhymes, or suggestive rhymes? Why, anyway, fold back a sentence or idea to get it into a prescribed arbitrary form? Why should we call this verse-tinkering and verse-shaping art, when it is only artifice? Why should we call the man who makes one pretty conceit rhyme with another pretty conceit an artist, and deny the term to the man whose sentences pair with great laws and forces?

Of course it is much easier for a poet to use the regular verse forms and verse language than it is to dispense with them; that is, a much less poetic capital is required in the former case than in the latter. The stock forms and the stock language count for a good deal. A very small amount of original talent may cut quite an imposing figure in the robes of the great masters. Require the poet to divest himself of them, and to speak in the language of men and in the spirit of real things, and see how he fares.

XV

Whitman was afraid of what he called the beauty disease. He thought a poet of the first order should be sparing of the direct use of the beautiful, as Nature herself is. His aim should be larger, and beauty should follow and not lead. The poet should not say to himself, " Come, I will make something beautiful," but rather " I will make something true, and quickening, and powerful. I will not dress my verse up in fine words and pretty fancies, but I will breathe into it the grit and force and adhesiveness of real things." Beauty is the flowering of life and fecundity, and it must have deep root in the non-beautiful.

Beauty, as the master knows it, is a spirit and not an adornment. It is not merely akin to flowers and gems and rainbows: it is akin to the All. Looking through his eyes, you shall see it in the rude and the savage also, in rocks and deserts and mountains, in the common as well as in the rare, in wrinkled age as well as in rosy youth.

The non-beautiful holds the world together, holds life together and nourishes it, more than the beautiful. Nature is beautiful because she is so much else first, — yes, and last, and all the time.

"For the roughness of the earth and of man encloses as
      much as the delicates of the earth and of man,
And nothing endures but personal qualities."

150

Is there not in field, wood, or shore something more precious and tonic than any special beauties we may chance to find there, — flowers, perfumes, sunsets, — something that we cannot do without, though we can do without these? Is it health, life, power, or what is it?

Whatever it is, it is something analogous to this that we get in Whitman. There is little in his "Leaves" that one would care to quote for its mere beauty, though this element is there also. One may pluck a flower here and there in his rugged landscape, as in any other; but the flowers are always by the way, and never the main matter. We should not miss them if they were not there. What delights and invigorates us is in the air, and in the look of things. The flowers are like our wild blossoms growing under great trees or amid rocks, never the camellia or tuberose of the garden or hothouse, — something rude and bracing is always present, always a breath of the untamed and aboriginal.

Whitman's work gives results, and never processes. There is no return of the mind upon itself; it descends constantly upon things, persons, realities. It is a rushing stream which will not stop to be analyzed. It has been urged that Whitman does not give the purely intellectual satisfaction that would seem to be warranted by his mental grasp and penetration. No, nor the æsthetic satisfaction

151

warranted by his essentially artistic habit of mind.
Well, he did not promise satisfaction in anything,
but only to put us on the road to satisfaction. His
book, he says, is not a "good lesson," but it lets
down the bars to a good lesson, and that to another,
and every one to another still.

Let me repeat that the sharp, distinct intellectual
note — the note of culture, books, clubs, etc., such
as we get from so many modern writers, you will
not get from Whitman. In my opinion, the note
he sounds is deeper and better than that. It has
been charged by an unfriendly critic that he strikes
lower than the intellect. If it is meant by this that
he misses the intellect, it is not true; he stimulates
the intellect as few poets do. He strikes lower
because he strikes farther. He sounds the note
of character, personality, volition, the note of prophecy, of democracy, and of love. He seems un-
intellectual to an abnormally intellectual age ; he
seems unpoetic to a taste formed upon poetic tidbits; he seems irreligious to standards founded
upon the old models of devotional piety; he seems
disorderly, incoherent to all petty thumb and fin-
ger measurements. In his ideas and convictions,
Whitman was a modern of the moderns; yet in his
type, his tastes, his fundamental make-up, he was
primitive, of an earlier race and age, — before, as
Emerson suggests, the gods had cut Man up into
men, with special talents of one kind or another.

XVI

Take any of Whitman's irregular-flowing lines, and clip and trim them, and compress them into artificial verse forms, and what have we gained to make up for what we have lost? Take his lines called "Reconciliation," for instance: —

"Word over all beautiful as the sky,

Beautiful that war and all its deeds of carnage must in
      time be utterly lost,

That the hands of the sisters Death and Night incessantly
      softly wash again, and ever again, this soil'd world;

For my enemy is dead, a man divine as myself is dead ;

I look where he lies white-faced and still in the coffin —
      I draw near,

Bend down, and touch lightly with my lips the white face
      in the coffin."

Or take his poem called "Old Ireland:" —

"Far hence amid an isle of wondrous beauty,

Crouching over a grave an ancient sorrowful mother,

Once a queen, now lean and tatter'd, seated on the ground,

Her old white hair drooping, dishevel'd, round her shoul-
      ders,

At her feet fallen an unused royal harp,

Long silent, she, too, long silent, mourning her shrouded
      hope and heir,

Of all the earth her heart most full of sorrow because
      most full of love.

"Yet a word, ancient mother,
You need crouch there no longer on the cold ground with
      forehead between your knees,
Oh, you need not sit there veil'd in your old white hair so
      dishevel'd,
For know you the one you mourn is not in that grave,
It was an illusion; the son you loved was not really dead,
The Lord is not dead, he is risen again young and strong
      in another country.
Even while you wept there by your fallen harp by the
      grave,
What you wept for was translated, pass'd from the grave,
The winds favor'd and the sea sail'd it,
And now with rosy and new blood,
Moves to-day in a new country."

Or take these lines from "Children of Adam:" —

"I heard you solemn-sweet pipes of the organ as last Sun-
      day morn I pass'd the church,
Winds of autumn, as I walk'd the woods at dusk I heard
      your long-stretch'd sighs up above so mournful,
I heard the perfect Italian tenor singing at the opera, I heard
      the soprano in the midst of the quartet singing;
Heart of my love! you, too, I heard murmuring low
      through one of the wrists around my head,
Heard the pulse of you, when all was still, ringing little
      bells last night under my ear."

Put such things as these, or in fact any of the poems,
in rhymed and measured verse, and you heighten a

certain effect, the effect of the highly wrought, the cunningly devised; but we lose just what the poet wanted to preserve at all hazards, — vista, unconstraint, the effect of the free-careering forces of nature.

I always think of a regulation verse form as a kind of corset which does not much disguise a good figure, though it certainly hampers it, and which is a great help to a poor figure. It covers up deficiencies, and it restrains exuberances. A personality like Whitman can wear it with ease and grace, as may be seen in a few of his minor poems, but for my part I like him best without it.

XVII

How well we know the language of the conventional poetic! In this language, the language of nine tenths of current poetry, the wind comes up out of the south and kisses the rose's crimson mouth, or it comes out of the wood and rumples the poppy's hood. Morning comes in glistening sandals, and her footsteps are jeweled with flowers. Everything is bedecked and bejeweled. Nothing is truly seen or truly reported. It is an attempt to paint the world beautiful. It is not beautiful as it is, and we must deck it out in the colors of the fancy. Now, I do not want the world painted for me. I want the grass green or brown, as the case may be; the sky blue, the rocks gray, the soil red;

and that the sun should rise and set without any poetic claptrap. What I want is to see these things spin around a thought, or float on the current of an emotion, as they always do in real poetry.

Beauty always follows, never leads the great poet. It arises out of the interior substance and structure of his work, like the bloom of health in the cheeks. The young poet thinks to win Beauty by direct and persistent wooing of her. He has not learned yet that she comes unsought to the truthful, the brave, the heroic. Let him think some great thought, experience some noble impulse, give himself with love to life and reality about him, and Beauty is already his. She is the reward of noble deeds.

XVIII

The modern standard in art is becoming more and more what has been called the canon of the characteristic, as distinguished from the Greek or classic canon of formal beauty. It is this canon, as Professor Triggs suggests, that we are to apply to Whitman. Dr. Johnson had it in mind when he wrote thus of Shakespeare: —

"The work of a correct and regular writer is a garden accurately formed and diligently planted, varied with shades and scented with flowers: the composition of Shakespeare is a forest in which oaks extend their branches, and pines tower in the air, interspersed sometimes with weeds and brambles, and sometimes giving shelter to myrtles and to roses; filling the eye with awful pomp, and gratifying the mind with endless diversity."

Classic art holds to certain fixed standards; it seeks formal beauty; it holds to order and proportion in external parts; its ideal of natural beauty is the well-ordered park or grove or flower-garden. It has a horror of the wild and savage. Mountains and forests, and tempests and seas, filled the classic mind with terror. Not so with the modern romantic mind, which finds its best stimulus and delight in free, unhampered nature. It loves the element of mystery and the suggestion of uncontrollable power. The modern mind has a sense of the vast, the infinite, that the Greek had not, and it is drawn by informal beauty more than by the formal.

XIX

It is urged against Whitman that he brings us the materials of poetry, but not poetry: he brings us the marble block, but not the statue; or he brings us the brick and mortar, but not the house. False or superficial analogies mislead us. Poetry is not something made; it is something grown, it is a vital union of the fact and the spirit. If the verse awakens in us the poetic thrill, the material, whatever it be, must have been touched with the transforming spirit of poesy. Why does Whitman's material suggest to any reader that it is poetic ma-

157

terial? Because it has already been breathed upon by the poetic spirit. A poet may bring the raw material of poetry in the sense that he may bring the raw material of a gold coin; the stamp and form you give it does not add to its value. It is doubtful if any of Whitman's utterances could be worked up into what is called poetry without a distinct loss of poetic value. What they would gain in finish they would lose in suggestiveness. This word "suggestiveness" affords one of the keys to Whitman. The objection to him I have been considering arises from the failure of the critic to see and appreciate his avowed purpose to make his page fruitful in poetic suggestion, rather than in samples of poetic elaboration. "I finish no specimens," he says. "I shower them by exhaustless laws, fresh and modern continually, as Nature does." He is quite content if he awaken the poetic emotion without at all satisfying it. He would have you more eager and hungry for poetry when you had finished with him than when you began. He brings the poetic stimulus, and brings it in fuller measure than any contemporary poet; and this is enough for him.

An eminent musician and composer, the late Dr. Ritter, told me that reading "Leaves of Grass" excited him to composition as no other poetry did. Tennyson left him passive and cold, but Whitman set his fingers in motion at once; he was so fruitful in themes, so suggestive of new harmonies and melodies. He gave the hints, and left his reader to follow them up. This is exactly what Whitman wanted to do. It defines his attitude toward poetry, toward philosophy, toward religion, — to suggest and set going, to arouse unanswerable questions, and to brace you to meet them; to bring the materials of poetry, if you will have it so, and leave you to make the poem; to start trains of thought, and leave you to pursue the flight alone. Not a thinker, several critics have urged; no, but the cause of thought in others to an unwonted degree. "Whether you agree with him or not," says an Australian essayist, "he will sting you into such an anguish of thought as must in the end be beneficial." It matters little to him whether or not you agree with him; what is important is, that you should think the matter out for yourself. He purposely avoids hemming you in by his conclusions; he would lead you in no direction but your own. "Once more I charge you give play to your self. I charge you leave all free, as I have left all free."

No thought, no philosophy, no music, no poetry, in his pages; no, it is all character, impulse, emotion, suggestion. But the true reader of him experiences all these things: he finds in his pages, if he knows how to look for it, a profound metaphysic, a profound ethic, a profound æsthetic; a theory of art and poetry which is never stated, but only hinted or suggested, and which is much more robust and vital than what we are used to; a theory of good and evil ; a view of character and conduct; a theory of the state and of politics, of the relation of the sexes, etc., to give ample food for thought and speculation. The Hegelian philosophy is in the "Leaves" as vital as the red corpuscles in the blood, so much is implied that is not stated, but only suggested, as in Nature herself. The really vast erudition of the work is adroitly concealed, hidden like its philosophy, as a tree hides its roots. Readers should not need to be told that, in the region of art as of religion, mentality is not first, but spirituality, personality, imagination; and that we do not expect a poet's thoughts to lie upon his pages like boulders in the field, but rather to show their presence like elements in the soil.

"Love-buds, put before you and within you, whoever you
     are,
Buds to be unfolded on the old terms,
If you bring the warmth of the sun to them, they will open,
     and bring form, color, perfume to you,
If you become the aliment and the wet, they will become
     flowers, fruits, tall branches and trees."

The early records and sacred books of most peoples contain what is called the materials of poetry. The Bible is full of such materials. English literature shows many attempts to work this material up into poetry, but always with a distinct loss of poetic value. The gold is simply beaten out thin and made to cover more surface, or it is mixed with some base metal. A recent English poet has attempted to work up the New Testament records into poetry, and the result is for the most part a thin, windy dilution of the original. If the record or legend is full of poetic suggestion, that is enough; to elaborate it, and deck it out in poetic finery without loss of poetic value, is next to impossible.

To me the Arthurian legends as they are given in the old books are more poetic, more stimulating to the imagination, than they are after they have gone through the verbal upholstering and polishing of such a poet as Swinburne or even Tennyson. These poets add little but words and flowers of fancy, and the heroic simplicity of the original is quite destroyed.

XX

No critic of repute has been more puzzled and misled by this unwrought character of our poet's verse than Mr. Edmund Gosse, the London poet and essayist. Mr. Gosse finds Whitman only a potential or possible poet; his work is literature in the condition of protoplasm. He is a maker of poems in solution; the structural change which should have crystallized his fluid and teeming pages into forms of art never came. It does not occur to Mr. Gosse to inquire whether or not something like this may not have been the poet's intention. Perhaps

161

this is the secret of the vitality of his work, which, as Mr. Gosse says, now, after forty years, shows no sign of declining. Perhaps it was a large, fresh supply of poetic yeast that the poet really sought to bring us. Undoubtedly Whitman aimed to give his work just this fluid, generative quality, to put into it the very basic elements of life itself. He feared the "structural change" to which Mr. Gosse refers; he knew it was more or less a change from life to death: the cell and not the crystal; the leaf of grass, and not the gem, is the type of his sentences. He sacrificed fixed form; above all, did he stop short of that conscious intellectual elaboration so characteristic of later poetry, the better to give the impression and the stimulus of creative elemental power. It is not to the point to urge that this is not the method or aim of other poets; that others have used the fixed forms, and found them plastic and vital in their hands. It was Whitman's aim; these were the effects he sought. I think beyond doubt that he gives us the impression of something dynamic, something akin to the vital forces of the organic world, much more distinctly and fully than any other poet who has lived.

Whitman always aimed to make his reader an active partner with him in his poetic enterprise. "I seek less," he says, "to state or display any theme or thought, and more to bring you, reader, into the atmosphere of the theme or thought, there to pur-

162

sue your own flight." This trait is brought out by Mr. Gosse in a little allegory. "Every reader who comes to Whitman," he says, "starts upon an expedition to the virgin forest. He must take his conveniences with him. He will make of the excursion what his own spirit dictates. [We generally do, in such cases, Mr. Gosse.] There are solitudes, fresh air, rough landscape, and a well of water, but if he wishes to enjoy the latter he must bring his own cup with him." This phase of Whitman's work has never been more clearly defined. Mr. Gosse utters it as an adverse criticism. It is true exposition, however we take it, what we get out of Whitman depends so largely upon what we bring to him. Readers will not all get the same. We do not all get the same out of a walk or a mountain climb. We get out of him in proportion to the sympathetic and interpretative power of our own spirits. Have you the brooding, warming, vivifying mother-mind? That vague, elusive, incommensurable something in the "Leaves" that led Symonds to say that talking about Whitman was like talking about the universe, — that seems to challenge our pursuit and definition, that takes on so many different aspects to so many different minds, — it seems to be this that has led Mr. Gosse to persuade himself that there is no real Walt Whitman, no man whom we can take, as we take any other figure in literature, as an "entity of positive value and definite characteristics," but a mere mass of literary protoplasm that takes the instant impression of whatever mood approaches it. Stevenson finds a Stevenson in it, Mr. Symonds finds a Symonds, Emerson finds an Emerson, etc. Truly may our poet say, "I contain multitudes." In what other poet do these men, or others like them, find themselves?

Whitman was a powerful solvent undoubtedly. He never hardens into anything like a system, or into mere intellectual propositions. One of his own phrases, "the fluid and swallowing soul," is descriptive of this trait of him. One source of his charm is, that we each see some phase of ourselves in him, as Mr. Gosse suggests. Above all things is he potential and indicative, bard of "flowing mouth and indicative hand." In his "Inscriptions" he says: —

"I am a man who, sauntering along without fully stopping, turns a casual look upon you and then averts his face,
Leaving it to you to prove and define it,
Expecting the main things from you."

This withholding and half-averted glancing, then, on the part of the poet, is deliberate and enters into the scheme of the work. Mr. Gosse would have shown himself a sounder critic had he penetrated the poet's purpose in this respect, and shown whether or not he had violated the canons he had set up for his own guidance. We do not condemn a creative work when it departs from some rule or precedent, but when it violates its own principle, when it is not consistent with itself, when it hath not eyes to see, or ears to hear, or hands to reach what lies within its own sphere. Art, in the plastic realms of written language, may set its mind upon elaboration, upon structural finish and proportion, upon exact forms and compensations, as in architecture, or it may set its mind upon suggestion, indirection, and the flowing, changing forms of organic nature. It is as much art in the one case as in the other. To get rid of all visible artifice is, of course, the great thing in both cases. There is so little apparent artifice in Whitman's case that he has been accused of being entirely without art, and of throwing his matter together in a haphazard way, — "without thought, without selection," without "composition, evolution, vertebration of style," says Mr. Gosse. Yet his work more than holds its own in a field where these things alone are supposed to insure success. Whitman covers up his processes well, and knows how to hit his mark without seeming to take aim. The verdicts upon him are mainly contradictory, because each critic only takes in a part of his scheme. Mr. Stedman finds him a formalist. Mr. Gosse finds in him a negation of all form. The London critic says he is without thought. A Boston critic speaks of what he happily calls the "waves of thought" in his work, — vast mind-impulses that lift and sway great masses of concrete facts and incidents. Whitman knew from the start that he would puzzle and baffle his critics, and would escape from them like air when they felt most sure they had him in their verbal nets. So it has been from the first, and so it continues to be. Without one thing, he says, it is useless to read him; and of what that one thing needful is, he gives only the vaguest hint, only a "significant look."

XXI

I may here notice two objections to Whitman urged by Mr. Stedman, — a critic for whose opinion I have great respect, and a man for whom I have a genuine affection. With all his boasted breadth and tolerance, Whitman, says my friend, is narrow; and with all his vaunted escape from the shackles of verse form, he is a formalist: his "irregular, manneristic chant" is as much at the extreme of artificiality as is the sonnet. These certainly are faults that one does not readily associate with the work of Whitman. But then I remember that the French critic, Scherer, charges Carlyle, the apostle of the gospel of sincerity, with being insincere and guilty of canting about cant. If Carlyle is insincere, I think it very likely that Whitman may be narrow and hide-bound. These things are so much a matter of temperament that one cannot judge for an-

other. Yet one ought not to confound narrowness
and breadth, or little and big. All earnest, uncompromising men are more or less open to the charge
of narrowness. A man is narrow when he concen-
trates himself upon a point; even a cannon-shot is.
Whitman was narrow in the sense that he was at
times monotonous; that he sought but few effects,
that he poured himself out mainly in one channel,
that he struck chiefly the major chords of life. His
"Leaves" do not show a great range of artistic
motifs. A versatile, many-sided nature he certainly
was not; a large, broad, tolerant nature he as certainly was. He does not assume many and diverse
forms like a purely artistic talent, sporting with and
masquerading in all the elements of life, like Shakespeare; but in his own proper form, and in his own
proper person, he gives a sense of vastness and
power that are unapproached in modern literature.
He asserts himself uncompromisingly, but he would
have you do the same. "He who spreads a wider
breast than my own proves the width of my own."
"He most honors my style who learns under it to
destroy the teacher." His highest hope is to be the
soil of superior poems.

Mr. Stedman thinks he detects in the poet a
partiality for the coarser, commoner elements of our
humanity over the finer and choicer, — for the
"rough" over the gentleman. But when all things
have been duly considered, it will be found, I think,

that he finally rests only with great personal qualities and traits. He is drawn by powerful, natural
persons, wherever found, — men and women self-
poised, fully equipped on all sides: —

"I announce a great individual, fluid as Nature, chaste,
    affectionate, compassionate, fully arm'd,
I announce a life that shall be copious, vehement, spiritual,
    bold," —

and much more to the same effect.

"I say nourish a great intellect, a great brain:
If I have said anything to the contrary, I hereby retract
    it."

Whitman is a formalist, just as every man who
has a way of his own of saying and doing things,
no matter how natural, is a formalist; but he is not
a stickler for form of any sort. He has his own
proper form, of course, which he rarely departs
from. At one extreme of artificiality Mr. Stedman
apparently places the sonnet. This is an arbitrary
form; its rules are inflexible; it is something cut
and shaped and fitted together after a predeter-
mined pattern, and to this extent is artificial. If
Whitman's irregularity was equally studied; if it
gave us the same sense of something cunningly
planned and wrought to a particular end, clipped
here, curbed there, folded back in this line, drawn
out in that, and attaining to a certain mechanical
proportion and balance as a whole, — then there

would be good ground for the critic's charge. But such is not the case. Whitman did not have, nor claim to have, the architectonic power of the great constructive poets. He did not build the lofty rhyme. He did not build anything, strictly speaking. He let himself go. He named his book after the grass, which makes a carpet over the earth, and which is a sign and a presence rather than a form.

XXII

Whitman's defects flow out of his great qualities. What we might expect from his size, his sense of mass and multitude, would be an occasional cumbrousness, turgidity, unwieldiness, ineffectualness: what we might expect from his vivid realism would be an occasional over-rankness or grossness; from his bluntness, a rudeness; from his passion for country, a little spread-eagleism; from his masterly use of indirection, occasional obscurity; from his mystic identification of himself with what is commonest, cheapest, nearest, a touch at times of the vulgar and unworthy; from his tremendous practical democracy, a bias at times toward too low an average; from his purpose "to effuse egotism and show it underlying all," may arise a little too much self-assertion. The price paid for his strenuousness and earnestness will be a want of humor; his determination to glorify the human body, as God made it, will bring him in collision with our notions

169

of the decent, the proper; the "courageous, clear
voice" with which he seeks to prove the sexual
organs and acts "illustrious," will result in his being
excluded from good society; his "heroic nudity"
will be apt to set the good dame, Belles-lettres, all
a-shiver; his healthful coarseness and godlike candor will put all the respectable folk to flight.

XXIII

To say that Whitman is a poet in undress is true
within certain limits. If it conveys the impression
that he is careless or inapt in the use of language,
or that the word is not always the fit word, the
best word, the saying does him injustice. No man
ever searched more diligently for the right word —
for just the right word — than did Whitman. He
would wait for days and weeks for the one ultimate
epithet. How long he pressed the language for
some word or phrase that would express the sense
of the evening call of the robin, and died without
the sight! But his language never obtrudes itself.
It has never stood before the mirror, it does not
consciously challenge your admiration, it is not obviously studied, it is never on dress parade. His
matchless phrases seem like chance hits, so much
so that some critics have wondered how he happened
to *stumble* upon them. His verse is not dressed
up, because it has so few of the artificial adjuncts
of poetry, — no finery or stuck-on ornament, —

nothing obtrusively beautiful or poetic; and because it bears itself with the freedom and nonchalance of a man in his every-day attire.

But it is always in a measure misleading to compare language with dress, to say that a poet clothes his thought, etc. The language is the thought; it is an incarnation, not an outside tailoring. To improve the expression is to improve the thought. In the most vital writing, the thought is nude; the mind of the reader touches something alive and real. When we begin to hear the rustle of a pompous or highly wrought vocabulary, when the man begins to dress his commonplace ideas up in fine phrases, we have enough of him.

Indeed, it is only the mechanical writer who may be said to " clothe " his ideas with words; the real poet thinks through words.

XXIV

I see that a plausible criticism might be made against Whitman, perhaps has been made, that in him we find the big merely, — strength without power, size without quality. A hasty reader might carry away this impression from his work, because undoubtedly one of the most obvious things about him is his great size. It is impossible not to feel that here is a large body of some sort. We have come upon a great river, a great lake, an immense plain, a rugged mountain. We feel that this mind

171

requires a large space to turn in. The page nearly always gives a sense of mass and multitude. All attempts at the playful or humorous seem ungainly. The style is processional and agglomerative. Out of these vast, rolling, cloud-like masses does there leap forth the true lightning? It seems to me there can be no doubt about that. The spirit easily triumphs. There is not only mass, there is penetration; not only vastness, there is sublimity; not only breadth, there is quality and charm. He is both Dantesque and Darwinian, as has been said.

Mr. Symonds was impressed with this quality of vastness in Whitman, and, despairing of conveying an adequate notion of him by any process of literary analysis, resorts to the use of a succession of metaphors, — the symbolic use of objects that convey the idea of size and power. Thus, "he is Behemoth, wallowing in primeval jungles;" "he is a gigantic elk or buffalo, trampling the grass of the wilderness;" "he is an immense tree, a kind of Ygdrasil, striking its roots deep down into the bowels of the world;" "he is the circumambient air in which float shadowy shapes, rise mirage-towers and palm-groves;" "he is the globe itself, — all seas, lands, forests, climates, storms, snows, sunshines, rains of universal earth."

Colonel Ingersoll said there was something in him akin to mountains and plains, and to the globe itself.

But Whitman is something more than a literary colossus. Pigmies can only claim pigmy honors. Size, after all, rules in this universe, because size and power go together. The large bodies rule the small. There is no impression of greatness in art without something that is analogous to size, — breadth, depth, height. The sense of vastness is never the gift of a minor poet. You cannot paint Niagara on the thumb-nail. Great artists are distinguished from small by the majesty of their conceptions.

Whitman's air is continental. He implies a big country, vast masses of humanity, sweeping and stirring times, the triumphs of science and the industrial age. He is the poet of mass and multitude. In his pages things are grouped and on the run, as it were. Little detail, little or no elaboration, little or no development of a theme, no minute studied effects so dear to the poets, but glimpses, suggestions, rapid surveys, sweeping movements, processions of objects, vista, vastness, — everywhere the effect of a man overlooking great spaces and calling off the significant and interesting points. He never stops to paint; he is contented to suggest. His "Leaves" are a rapid, joyous survey of the forces and objects of the universe, first with reference to character and personality, and next with reference to America and democracy. His method of treatment is wholesale and accumulative. It is typified by this passage in his first poem: —

"Listen! I will be honest with you,
I do not offer the old smooth prizes, but offer rough new
    prizes.

"I tramp a perpetual journey,
My signs are a rain-proof coat, good shoes, and a staff
    cut from the woods,
No friend of mine takes his ease in my chair,
I have no chair, no church, no philosophy,
I lead no man to a dinner table, library, or exchange,
But each man and each woman of you I lead upon a knoll,
My left hand hooking you round the waist,
My right hand pointing to landscapes of continents and a
    plain public road."

He deals with the major elements of life, and
always aims at large effects. "Lover of populous
pavements," he is occupied with large thoughts and
images, with races, eras, multitudes, processions.
His salute is to the world. He keeps the whole
geography of his country and of the globe before
him; his purpose in his poems spans the whole
modern world. He views life as from some emi-
nence from which many shades and differences disappear. He sees things in mass. Many of our
cherished conventions disappear from his point of
view. He sees the fundamental and necessary
things. His vision is sweeping and final. He tries
himself by the orbs. His standards of poetry and
art are astronomic. He sees his own likeness in the

earth. His rapture springs, not so much from the contemplation of bits and parts as from the contemplation of the whole. There is a breadth of sympathy and of interest that does not mind particulars. He says: —

"It is no small matter, this round and delicious globe,
        moving so exactly in its orbit forever and ever,
        without one jolt, or the untruth of a single second,
I do not think it was made in six days, nor in ten thousand years, nor ten billions of years,
Nor planned and built one thing after another as an architect plans and builds a house."

In old age he sees "the estuary that enlarges and spreads itself grandly as it pours into the sea." He looks upon all things at a certain remove. These are typical lines: —

"A thousand perfect men and women appear,
Around each gathers a cluster of friends, and gay children
        and youths, with offerings.

"Women sit, or move to and fro, some old, some young,
The young are beautiful — but the old are more beautiful
        than the young."

"The Runner," "A Farm Picture," and scores of others, are to the same effect. Always wholes, total impressions, — always a view as of a "strong bird on pinion free." Few details, but panoramic effects; not the flower, but the landscape; not a tree, but a forest; not a street corner, but a city. The title of one of his poems, "A Song of the Rolling Earth," might stand as the title of the book. When he gathers details and special features he masses them like a bouquet of herbs and flowers. No cameo carving, but large, bold, rough, heroic sculpturing. The poetry is always in the totals, the breadth, the sweep of conception. The part that is local, specific, genre, near at hand, is Whitman himself; his personality is the background across which it all flits.

We make a mistake when we demand of Whitman what the other poets give us, — studies, embroidery, delicate tracings, pleasing artistic effects, rounded and finished specimens. We shall understand him better if we inquire what his own standards are, what kind of a poet he would be. He tells us over and over again that he would emulate the great forces and processes of Nature. He seeks for hints in the sea, the mountain, in the orbs themselves. In the wild splendor and savageness of a Colorado canyon he sees a spirit kindred to his own.

He dwells fondly, significantly, upon the amplitude, the coarseness, and what he calls the sexuality, of the earth, and upon its great charity and equilibrium.

"The earth," he says, "does not withhold; it is generous enough: —

"The truths of the earth continually wait, they are not so concealed either,

They are calm, subtle, untransmissible by print.

They are imbued through all things, conveying themselves willingly,

Conveying a sentiment and invitation of the earth — I
utter and utter!"

. . . .

"The earth does not argue,

Is not pathetic, has no arrangements,

Does not scream, haste, persuade, threaten, promise,

Makes no discriminations, has no conceivable failures,

Closes nothing, refuses nothing, shuts none out.

Of all the powers, objects, states, it notifies, shuts none
out."

He says the best of life

"Is not what you anticipated — it is cheaper, easier,
nearer,"

and that the earth affords the final standard of all
things: —

"I swear there can be no theory of any account unless it
corroborate the theory of the earth,

No politics, art, religion, behavior, or what not, is of
account unless it compares with the amplitude of
the earth,

Unless it face the exactness, vitality, impartiality, rectitude, of the earth."

No one can make a study of our poet without
being deeply impressed with these and kindred passages: —

"The maker of poems settles justice, reality, immortality,
His insight and power encircle things and the human race.

WHITMAN

The singers do not beget, only the Poet begets,
The singers are welcom'd, understood, appear often
    enough, but rare has the day been, likewise the spot,
    of the birth of the maker of poems, the Answerer
(Not every century, nor every five centuries has contain'd
    such a day, for all its names).

.   .   .   .

"All this time and at all times wait the words of true
    poems,
The words of true poems do not merely please,
The true poets are not followers of beauty, but the august
    masters of beauty;
The greatness of sons is the exuding of the greatness of
    mothers and fathers,
The words of true poems are the tuft and final applause of
    science.

"Divine instinct, breadth of vision, the law of reason,
    health, rudeness of body, withdrawnness,
Gayety, sun-tan, air-sweetness, such are some of the
    words of poems,
The sailor, the traveler, underlie the maker of poems, the
    Answerer,
The builder, geometer, chemist, anatomist, phrenologist,
    artist, all these underlie the maker of poems, the
    Answerer.
The words of the true poems give you more than poems;
They give you to form for yourself poems, religions, poli-
    tics, war, peace, behavior, histories, essays, daily
    life, and everything else.

They balance ranks, colors, races, creeds, and the sexes;
They do not seek beauty, they are sought;
Forever touching them or close upon them follows beauty,
longing, fain, love-sick.
They prepare for death, yet are they not the finish, but
rather the outset,
They bring none to his or her terminus or to be contented
and full,
Whom they take they take into space to behold the birth
of stars, to learn one of the meanings,
To launch off with absolute faith, to sweep through the
ceaseless rings and never be quiet again.

.   .   .   .

"Of these States the poet is the equable man,
Not in him but off from him things are grotesque, eccen-
tric, fail of their full returns,
Nothing out of its place is good, nothing in its place is bad,
He bestows on every object or quality its fit proportion,
neither more nor less,
He is the arbiter of the diverse, he is the key,
He is the equalizer of his age and land,
He supplies what wants supplying, he checks what wants
checking,
In peace out of him speaks the spirit of peace, large, rich,
thrifty, building populous towns, encouraging
agriculture, arts, commerce, lighting the study of
man, the soul, health, immortality, government,
In war he is the best backer of the war, he fetches artillery
as good as the engineer's, he can make every word
he speaks draw blood,

The years straying toward infidelity he withholds by his
  steady faith,
He is no arguer, he is judgment (nature accepts him ab-
  solutely),
He judges not as the judge judges, but as the sun falling
  round a helpless thing,
As he sees the farthest he has the most faith,
His thoughts are the hymns of the praise of things,
In the dispute on God and eternity he is silent,
He sees eternity less like a play with a prologue and de-
  nouement,
He sees eternity in men and women, he does not see men
  and women as dreams or dots.

.   .   .   .

"Rhymes and rhymers pass away, poems distill'd from
  other poems pass away,
The swarms of reflectors and the polite pass, and leave
  ashes,
Admirers, impostors, obedient persons, make but the
  soil of literature."

Folded up in these sentences, often many times
folded up, is Whitman's idea of the poet, the begetter, the reconciler; not the priest of the beautiful, but the master of the All, who does not appear
once in centuries.

We hear nothing of the popular conception of the
poet, well reflected in these lines of Tennyson: —

"The poet in a golden clime was born, with golden stars
  above."

"Golden stars" and "golden climes" do not figure at all in Whitman's pages; the spirit of romance is sternly excluded.

Whitman's ideal poet is the most composite man, rich in temperament, rank in the human attributes, embracing races and eras in himself. All men see themselves in him: —

"The mechanic takes him for a mechanic,
And the soldier supposes him to be a soldier, and the sailor
      that he has followed the sea,
And the authors take him for an author, and the artists
      for an artist,
And the laborers perceive he could labor with them and
      love them,
No matter what the work is, that he is the one to follow it,
      or has followed it,
No matter what the nation, that he might find his brothers
      and sisters there.

. . . .

"The gentleman of perfect blood acknowledges his perfect
      blood,
The insulter, the prostitute, the angry person, the beggar,
      see themselves in the ways of him, he strangely
      transmutes them,
They are not vile any more, they hardly know themselves
      they are so grown."

Let us hold the poet to his own ideals, and not condemn him because he has not aimed at something foreign to himself.

WHITMAN

The questions which Whitman puts to him who would be an American poet may fairly be put to himself.

"Are you faithful to things? Do you teach what the land and sea, the bodies of men, womanhood, amativeness, heroic angers, teach?

Have you sped through fleeting customs, popularities?

Can you hold your hand against all seductions, follies, whirls, fierce contentions? are you very strong? are you really of the whole people?

Are you not of some coterie? some school, or mere religion?

Are you done with reviews and criticisms of life? animating now to life itself?

Have you vivified yourself from the maternity of these States?

Have you, too, the old, ever-fresh forbearance and impartiality?

. . . .

What is this you bring my America?

Is it uniform with my country?

Is it not something that has been better done or told before?

Have you not imported this or the spirit of it in some ship?

Is it not a mere tale? a rhyme? a pettiness? — is the good old cause in it?

Has it not dangled long at the heels of the poets, politicians, literats of enemies' lands?

Does it not assume that what is notoriously gone is still here?

Does it answer universal needs? will it improve manners?

Can your performance face the open fields and the seaside?

Will it absorb into me as I absorb food, air, to appear
again in my strength, gait, face?

Have real employments contributed to it? Original mak-
ers, not mere amanuenses?"

So far as Whitman's poetry falls within any of
the old divisions it is lyrical, — a personal and individual utterance. Open the book anywhere and
you are face to face with a man. His eye is fixed
upon you. It is a man's voice you hear, and it is
directed to *you*. He is not elaborating a theme: he
is suggesting a relation or hinting a meaning. He is
not chiseling, or carving a work of art: he is roughly
outlining a man; he is planting a seed, or tilling a
field.

XXV

I believe it was the lamented Professor Clifford
who first used the term "cosmic emotion" in connection with "Leaves of Grass." Whitman's atmosphere is so distinctly outside of and above that
which ministers to our social and domestic wants, —
the confined and perfumed air of an indoor life;
his mood and temper are so habitually begotten by
the contemplation of the orbs and the laws and
processes of universal nature, that the phrase often
comes to mind in considering him. He is not in any

sense, except perhaps in a few minor pieces, a domestic and fireside poet, — a solace to our social
instincts and cultivated ideals. He is too large, too
aboriginal, too elemental, too strong for that. I seem
to understand and appreciate him best when I keep
in mind the earth as a whole, and its relation to
the system. Any large view or thought, or survey of
life or mankind, is a preparation for him. He demands the outdoor temper and habit, he demands
a sense of space and power, he demands above all
things a feeling for reality. "Vastness" is a word
that applies to him; abysmal man, cosmic consciousness, the standards of the natural universal,
— all hint some phase of his genius. His survey of
life and duty is from a point not included in any
four walls, or in any school or convention. It is a
survey from out the depths of being; the breath of
worlds and systems is in these utterances. His treatment of sex, of comradeship, of death, of democracy, of religion, of art, of immortality, is in the
spirit of the great out-of-doors of the universe; the
point of view is cosmic rather than personal or phi-
lanthropic. What charity is this! — the charity of
sunlight that spares nothing and turns away from
nothing. What "heroic nudity"! like the naked-
ness of rocks and winter trees. What sexuality! like
the lust of spring or the push of tides. What welcome to death, as only the night which proves the
day!

XXVI

This orbic nature which so thrills and fills Whitman is not at all akin to that which we get in the so-called nature poets of Wordsworth and his school, — the charm of privacy, of the sequestered, the cosy, — qualities that belong to the art of a domestic, home-loving race, and to lovers of solitude. Tennyson's poetry abounds in these qualities; so does Wordsworth's. There is less of them in Browning, and more of them in the younger poets. That communing with nature, those dear friendships with birds and flowers, that gentle wooing of the wild and sylvan, that flavor of the rural, the bucolic, — all these are important features in the current popular poetry, but they are not to any marked extent characteristic of Whitman. The sentiment of domesticity, love as a sentiment; the attraction of children, home, and fireside; the attraction of books, art, travel; our pleasure in the choice, the refined, the artificial, — these are not the things you are to demand of Whitman. You do not demand them of Homer or Dante or the Biblical writers. We are to demand of him the major things, primary things; the lift of great emotions; the cosmic, the universal; the joy of health, of selfhood; the stimulus of the real, the modern, the American; always the large, the virile; always perfect acceptance and triumph.

Whitman's free use of the speech of the common

185

people is doubtless offensive to a fastidious literary taste. Such phrases as "I will be even with you," "what would it amount to," "give in," "not one jot less;" "young fellows," "old fellows," "stuck up," "every bit as much," "week in and week out," and a thousand others, would jar on the page of any other poet more than on his.

XXVII

William Rossetti says his language has a certain ultimate quality. Another critic speaks of his absolute use of language. Colonel Ingersoll credits him with more supreme words than have been uttered by any other man of our time.

The power to use words was in Whitman's eyes a divine power, and was bought with a price: —

"For only at last after many years, after chastity, friend-
    ship, procreation, prudence, and nakedness,
After treading ground, and breasting river and lake,
After a loosen'd throat, after absorbing eras, tempera-
    ments, races, after knowledge, freedom, crimes,
After complete faith, after clarifying elevations and re-
    moving obstructions,
After these and more, it is just possible there comes to a
    man, a woman, the divine power to speak words."

Whitman's sense of composition and his rare artistic faculty of using language are seen, as John Addington Symonds says, in the "countless clear

and perfect phrases" "which are hung, like golden
medals of consummate workmanship and incised
form, in rich clusters over every poem he produced.
And, what he aimed at above all, these phrases are
redolent of the very spirit of the emotions they suggest, communicate the breadth and largeness of the
natural things they indicate, embody the essence
of realities in living words which palpitate and burn
forever."

The great poet is always more or less the original,
the abysmal man. He is face to face with universal
laws and conditions. He speaks out of a greater
exaltation of sentiment than the prose-writer. He
takes liberties; he speaks for all men; he is a bird
on "pinions free."

XXVIII

In saying or implying that Whitman's aim was
not primarily literary or artistic, I am liable to be
misunderstood; and when Whitman himself says,
"No one will get at my verses who insists upon
viewing them as a literary performance, or attempt
at such performance, or as aiming mainly toward
art or æstheticism," he exposes himself to the same
misconception. It is the literary and poetic value
of his verses alone that can save them. Their philosophy, their democracy, their vehement patriotism,
their religious ardor, their spirit of comradeship, or
what not, will not alone suffice. All depends upon

the manner in which these things are presented to us. Do we get the reality, or words about the reality? No matter what the content of the verse, unless into the whole is breathed the breath of the true creative artist they will surely perish. Oblivion awaits every utterance not touched with the life of the spirit. Whitman was as essentially an artist as was Shakespeare or Dante; his work shows the same fusion of imagination, will, emotion, personality; it carries the same quality of real things, — not the same shaping, constructive power, but the same quickening, stimulating power, the same magic use of words. The artist in him is less conscious of itself, is less differentiated from the man, than in the other poets. He objected to having his work estimated for its literary value alone, but in so doing he used the word in a narrow sense.

After all these ages of the assiduous cultivation of literature, there has grown up in men a kind of lust of the mere art of writing, just as, after so many generations of religious training, there has grown up a passion for religious forms and observances. "Mere literature" has come to be a current phrase in criticism, meaning, I suppose, that the production to which it is applied is notable only for good craftsmanship. In the same spirit one speaks of mere scholarship, or of a certain type of man as a mere gentleman. It was mere literature that Whitman was afraid of, the æsthetic disease, the passion for letters, for poetry, divorced from love of life and of things. None knew better than he that the ultimate value of any imaginative and emotional work, even of the Bible, is its literary value. Its spiritual and religious value is inseparably connected with its literary value.

"Leaves of Grass" is not bookish; it is always the voice of a man, and not of a scholar or conventional poet, that addresses us. We all imbue words more or less with meanings of our own; but, from the point of view I am now essaying, literature is the largest fact, and embraces all inspired utterances. The hymn-book seeks to embody or awaken religious emotion alone; would its religious value be less if its poetic value were more? I think not. The best of the Psalms of David, from the religious point of view, are the best from the literary point of view. What reaches and thrills the soul, — that is great art. What arouses the passions — mirth, anger, indignation, pity — may or may not be true art. No one, for instance, can read "Uncle Tom's Cabin" without tears, laughter, anger; but no one, I fancy, could ever get from it that deep, tranquil pleasure and edification that the great imaginative works impart. Keble's poetry is more obviously religious than Wordsworth's or Arnold's, but how short-lived, because it is not embalmed in the true artistic spirit! In all the great poems, there is something as deep and calm as the light and the sky, and as common and universal. I find this something in Whitman. In saying, therefore, that his aim was ulterior to that of art, that he was not begotten by the literary spirit, I only mean that his aim was that of the largest art, and of the most vital and comprehensive literature. We should have heard the last of his "Leaves" long ago had they not possessed unmistakably the vitality of true literature, "incomparable things, incomparably well said," as Emerson remarked.

A scientific or philosophical work lives independently of its literary merit, but an emotional and imaginative work lives only by virtue of its literary merit. Different meanings may be attached to these words "literary merit" by different persons. I use them as meaning that vital and imaginative use of language which is the characteristic of all true literature. The most effective way of saying a thing in the region of the sentiments and emotions, — that is the true literary way.

HIS RELATION TO LIFE AND
MORALS

I

I HAVE divided my subject into many chapters, and given to each a separate heading, yet I am aware that they are all but slight variations of a single theme, — viz., Whitman's reliance upon absolute nature. That there might be no mistake about it, and that his reader might at once be put in possession of his point of view, the poet declared at the outset of his career that at every hazard he should let nature speak.

"Creeds and schools in abeyance
Retiring back awhile, sufficed at what they are, but never
  forgotten,
I harbor for good or bad,
I permit to speak at every hazard,
Nature without check, with original energy."

The hazard of letting nature speak will, of course, be great, — the hazard of gross misapprehension on the part of the public, and of hesitancy and inadequacy on the part of the poet. The latter danger, I think, was safely passed; Whitman never flinched or wavered for a moment, and that his criticism is

191

adequate seems to me equally obvious. But the former contingency — the gross misapprehension of the public, even the wiser public — has been astounding. He has been read in a narrow, literal, bourgeois spirit. The personal pronoun, which he uses so freely, has been taken to stand for the private individual Walt Whitman, so that he has been looked upon as a compound of egotism and licentiousness. His character has been traduced, and his purpose in the "Leaves" entirely misunderstood.

We see at a glance that his attitude towards nature, towards God, towards the body and the soul, reverses many of the old ascetic theological conceptions.

All is good, all is as it should be; to abase the body is to abase the soul. Man is divine inside and out, and is no more divine about the head than about the loins. It is from this point of view that he has launched his work. He believed the time had come for an utterance out of radical, uncompromising human nature; let conventions and refinements stand back, let nature, let the soul, let the elemental forces speak; let the body, the passions, sex, be exalted; the stone rejected by the builders shall be the chief stone in the corner. Evil shall be shown to be a part of the good, and death shall be welcomed as joyously as life.

Whitman says his poems will do just as much evil as good, and perhaps more. To many readers this confession of itself would be his condemnation. To others it would be an evidence of his candor and breadth of view. I suppose all great vital forces, whether embodied in a man or in a book, work evil as well as good. If they do not, they only tickle the surface of things. Has not the Bible worked evil also? Some think more evil than good. The dews and the rains and the sunshine work evil.

From Whitman's point of view, there is no good without evil; evil is an unripe kind of good. There is no light without darkness, no life without death, no growth without pain and struggle. Beware the emasculated good, the good by exclusion rather than by victory. "Leaves of Grass" will work evil on evil minds, — on narrow, unbalanced minds. It is not a guide, but an inspiration; not a remedy, but health and strength. Art does not preach directly but indirectly; it is moral by its spirit, and the mood and temper it begets.

Whitman, in celebrating manly pride, self-reliance, the deliciousness of sex; in glorifying the body, the natural passions and appetites, nativity; in identifying himself with criminals and low or lewd persons; in frankly imputing to himself all sins men are guilty of, runs the risk, of course, of being read in a spirit less generous and redemptive than his own.

The charity of the poet may stimulate the license of the libertine; the optimism of the seer may confirm the evil-doer; the equality of the democrat may foster the insolence of the rowdy. This is our lookout and not the poet's. We take the same chances with him that we do with nature; we are to trim our sails to the breeze he brings; we are to sow wheat and not tares for his rains to water.

Whitman's glorification of the body has led some critics to say that he is the poet of the body only. But it is just as true to say he is the poet of the soul only. He always seeks the spiritual through the material. He treats the body and the soul as one, and he treats all things as having reference to the soul.

"I will not make a poem, nor the least part of a poem, but
     has reference to the soul,
Because, having look'd at the objects of the universe, I
     find there is no one, nor any particle of one, but
     has reference to the soul."

The curious physiological strain which runs through the poems is to be considered in the light of this idea. He exalts the body because in doing so he exalts the soul.

"Sure as the earth swims through the heavens, does every
     one of its objects pass into spiritual results."

II

The reader of Whitman must do his or her own moralizing; the poet is here not to deprecate or criticise, but to love and celebrate; he has no partialities; our notions of morality do not concern him; he exploits the average man just as he finds him; he *is* the average man for the time being and confesses to all his sins and shortcomings, and we will make of the result good or evil, according to our mental horizon. That his work is unmixed good is the last thing the poet would claim for it. He has not, after the easy fashion of the moralist, set the good here and the bad there; he has blended them as they are in nature and in life; our profit and discipline begin when we have found out whither he finally tends, or when we have mastered him and extracted the good he holds. If we expect he is going to preach an austere system of morality to us, or any system of morality, we are doomed to disappointment. Does Nature preach such a system? does Nature preach at all? neither will he. He presents you the elements of good and evil in himself in vital fusion and play; your part is to see how the totals are at last good.

It is objected that Whitman is too persistent in declaring himself an animal, when the thing a man is least likely to forget is that he is an animal and the thing he is least likely to remember is that he is a spirit and a child of God. But Whitman insists with the same determination that he is a spirit and an heir of immortality, — not as one who has cheated the devil of his due, but as one who shares the privileges and felicities of all, and who finds the divine in the human. Indeed it is here that he sounds his most joyous and triumphant note. No such faith in spiritual results, no such conviction of the truth of immortality, no such determined recognition of the unseen world as the final reality is to be found in modern poetry.

As I have said, Whitman aimed to put his whole nature in a poem — the physical or physiological, the spiritual, the æsthetic and intellectual, — without giving any undue prominence to either. If he has not done so, if he has made the animal and sexual too pronounced, more so than nature will justify in the best proportioned man, then and then only is his artistic scheme vitiated and his work truly immoral.

It may be true that the thing a man is least likely to forget is that he is an animal; what he is most likely to forget, is that the animal is just as sacred and important as any other part; indeed that it is the basis of all, and that a sane and healthful and powerful spirituality and intellectuality can only flow out of a sane and healthful animality.

"I believe in you, my soul, the other I am must not abase
    itself to you,
And you must not be abased to the other."

III

Furthermore, Whitman's main problem is to project into literature the new democratic man as he

196

conceives him, — the man of the future, intensely
American, but in the broadest sense human and
cosmopolitan; he is to project him on a scale large
enough for all uses and conditions, ignoring the
feudal and aristocratic types which have for the
most part dominated literature, and matching them
with a type more copious in friendship, charity,
sympathy, religion, candor, and of equal egoism and
power.

It is to exploit and enforce and illustrate this
type of character that "Leaves of Grass" is written. The poems are the drama of this new democratic man. This type Whitman finds in himself.
He does not have to create it as Shakespeare did
Hamlet or Lear; he has only to discover it in himself. He is it and he gives it free utterance. His
work is, therefore, as he says, the poem of himself,
— himself written large, — written as upon the face
of the continent, written in the types and events he
finds on all sides. He sees himself in all men, the
bad as well as the good, and he sees all men in himself. All the stupendous claims he makes for himself he makes for others. His egotism is vicarious and embraces the world. It is not the private
individual Walt Whitman that makes these stupendous claims for himself; it is Walt Whitman as the
spokesman of the genius of American democracy.
He is not to discuss a question. He is to outline a
character, he is to incarnate a principle. The essay-

ist or philosopher may discuss the value of any given idea, — may talk about it; the creative artist alone can give us the thing itself, the concrete flesh-and-blood reality. Whitman is not only to make this survey, to launch this criticism; he is to embody it in a living human personality, and enable us to see the world of man and morals through its eyes. What with the scientist, the philosopher, is thought, must be emotion and passion with him.

Whitman promises that we shall share with him "two greatnesses, and a third one rising inclusive and more resplendent," —

"The greatness of Love and Democracy and the greatness of Religion," —

not merely as ideas, but as living impulses. He is to show the spirit of absolute, impartial nature, incarnated in a human being, imbued with love, democracy, and religion, moving amid the scenes and events of the New World, sounding all the joys and abandonments of life, and re-reading the oracles from the American point of view. And the utterance launched forth is to be imbued with poetic passion.

Whitman always aims at a complete human synthesis, and leaves his reader to make of it what he can. It is not for the poet to qualify and explain. He seeks to reproduce his whole nature in a book, — reproduce it with all its contradictions and carnalities, the good and the bad, the coarse and the fine, the body and the soul, — to give free swing to himself, trusting to natural checks and compensations to insure a good result at last, but not at all disturbed if you find parts of it bad as in creation itself.

His method being that of the poet, and not that of the moralist or preacher, how shall he sort and sift, culling this virtue and that, giving parts and fragments instead of the entire man ? He must give all, not abstractly, but concretely, synthetically.

To a common prostitute Whitman says: —

"Not till the sun excludes you do I exclude you;
Not till the waters refuse to glisten for you, and the leaves
　　to rustle for you, do my words refuse to glisten and
　　rustle for you."

We are housed in social usages and laws, we are sheltered and warmed and comforted by conventions and institutions and numberless traditions; their value no one disputes. But for purposes of his own Whitman ignores them all; he lets in upon us the free and maybe raw air of the great out-of-doors of absolute nature; his standards are not found inside of any four walls; he contemplates life, and would quicken it in its fundamentals; his survey is from a plane whence our arts and refinements and petty distinctions disappear. He sees the evil of the world no less necessary than the good;

he sees death as a part of life itself; he sees the
body and the soul as one; he sees the spiritual
always issuing from the material; he sees not one
result at last lamentable in the universe.

IV

Unless, as I have already said, we allow Whitman to be a law unto himself, we can make little of
him; unless we place ourselves at his absolute point
of view, his work is an offense and without meaning. The only question is, Has he a law, has he
a steady and rational point of view, is his work a
consistent and well-organized whole? Ask yourself, What is the point of view of absolute, uncompromising science? It is that creation is all good
and sound; things are as they should be or must be;
there are no conceivable failures; there is no evil
in the final analysis, or, if there is, it is necessary,
and plays its part also; there is no more beginning
nor ending than there is now, no more heaven or
hell than we find or make here: —

"Did you guess the celestial laws are yet to be work'd
over and rectified?"

It has been urged that Whitman violates his own
canon of the excellence of nature. But what he
violates is more a secondary or acquired nature.
He violates our social conventions and instincts, he
exposes what we cover up; but the spirit of his

undertaking demanded this of him. Remember that at all hazards he is to let nature — absolute nature — speak; that he is to be the poet of the body as well as of the soul, and that no part of the body of a man or woman, "hearty and clean," is vile, and that "none shall be less familiar than the rest."

His glory is, that he never flinched or hesitated in following his principle to its logical conclusions, — "my commission obeying, to question it never daring."

It was an heroic sacrifice, and atones for the sins of us all, — the sins of perverting, denying, abusing the most sacred and important organs and functions of our bodies.

v

In Whitman we find the most complete identification of the man with the subject. He always is, or becomes, the thing he portrays. Not merely does he portray America, — he speaks out of the American spirit, the spirit that has broken irrevocably with the past and turns joyously to the future; he does not praise equality, he illustrates it; he puts himself down beside the lowest and most despised person, and calls him brother.

"You felons on trial in courts,
You convicts in prison-cells, you sentenced assassins
    chain'd and handcuff'd with iron,
Who am I too that I am not on trial or in prison?

201

Me ruthless and devilish as any, that my wrists are not
    chain'd with iron or my ankles with iron?"

He does not give a little charity, he gives himself as freely as the clouds give rain, or the sun gives
light; he does not write a treatise on democracy, he
applies the democratic spirit to everything in heaven and on earth, and redistributes the prizes from
its points of view; he does not, except very briefly,
sing the praises of science, but he launches his poems
always from the scientific view of the world, in
contradistinction to the old theological and myth-
ical point of view. It is always the example, it is
always the thing itself, he gives us. Few precepts,
no sermon, no reproof. Does he praise candor? No,
he is candor; he confesses to everything; he shows
us the inmost working of his mind. We know him
better than we know our nearest friends. Does he
exalt the pride of man in himself, or egoism? Again
he illustrates it: he is egoism; he makes the whole
universe revolve around himself; he never for a
moment goes out of himself; he does not seek a
theme; he is the theme. His egocentric method of
treatment is what characterizes him as an artist.
He elaborates no theme, he builds nothing, he carves
nothing, but makes himself a source and centre
of pulsing, vital energy. Wave after wave radiates
from him. What we see and get always is Walt
Whitman. Our attention is never fixed upon the
writer, but always upon the man.

Of course this method of Whitman of becoming one with his subject, and speaking out of it, is always the method of the creative artist. It is this that distinguishes the artist from the mere thinker or prose-writer. The latter tells us about a thing; the former gives us the thing, or the spirit of the thing itself.

If Whitman had put his criticism of our time and civilization in an argument or essay, the world would have received it very differently. As an intellectual statement or proposition, we could have played with it and tossed it about as a ball in a game of shuttlecock, and dropped it when we tired of it, as we do other criticism. But he gave it to us as a man, as a personality, and we find it too strong for us. It is easier to deal with a theory than with the concrete reality. A man is a summons and a challenge, and will not be easily put aside.

The great philosophical poets, like Lucretius, try to solve the riddles. Whitman's aim is only to thrust the riddles before you, to give you a new sense of them, and start the game afresh. He knows what a complex, contradictory thing the universe is, and that the most any poet can do is to break the old firmament up into new forms. To put his arms around it? No. Put your arms around your fellow-man, and then you have encompassed it as nearly as mortal can do.

VI

Whitman's attraction toward the common people was real. There is one thing that makes every-day humanity, the great, toiling, unlettered masses, forever welcome to men who unite great imagination with broad sympathies, — they give a sense of reality; they refresh, as nature always refreshes. There is a tang and a sting to the native, the spontaneous, that the cultivated rarely has. The farmer, the mechanic, the sailor, the soldier, savor of the primal and the hardy. In painting his own portrait, Whitman makes prominent the coarser, unrefined traits, because here the colors are fast, — here is the basis of all. The careful student of Whitman will surely come to see how all the elements of his picture — his pride, his candor, his democracy, his sensuality, his coarseness — finally fit together, and correct and offset one another and make a perfect unity.

No poet is so easily caricatured and turned into ridicule as Whitman. He is deficient in humor, and hence, like the Biblical writers, is sometimes on the verge of the grotesque without knowing it. The sense of the ridiculous has been enormously stimulated and developed in the modern mind, and — what is to be regretted — it has been mostly at the expense of the sense of awe and reverence. We "poke fun" at everything in this country; to whatever approaches the verge of the ridiculous we give a push and topple it over. The fear which all Americans have before their eyes, and which is much stronger than the fear of purgatory, is the fear of appearing ridiculous. We curb and check any eccentricity or marked individuality of manners or dress, lest we expose ourselves to the shafts of ridicule. Emerson said he had heard with admiring submission the remark of a lady who declared that the sense of being perfectly well dressed gave a feeling of inward tranquillity which religion was powerless to bestow; and what ranks before religion with us as a people is being in the mode, and writing our verse and cutting our coats in the approved style. Pride of the eye, a keen sense of the proprieties and the conventionalities, and a morbid feeling for the ridiculous, would have been death to Whitman's undertaking. He would have faltered, or betrayed self-consciousness. He certainly never could have spoken with that elemental aplomb and indifference which is so marked a feature of his work. Any hesitation, any knuckling, would have been his ruin. We should have seen he was not entirely serious, and should have laughed at him. We laugh now only for a moment; the spell of his earnestness and power is soon upon us.

VII

Thoreau considered Whitman's "Leaves" worth all the sermons in the country for preaching; and yet few poets have assumed so little the function of the preacher. His great cure-all is love; he gives himself instead of a sermon. His faith in the remedial power of affection, comradeship, is truly Christ-like. Lover of sinners is also his designation. The reproof is always indirect or implied. He brings to bear character rather than precept. He helps you as health, as nature, as fresh air, pure water help. He says to you:—

" The mockeries are not you;
Underneath them, and within them, I see you lurk;
I pursue you where none else has pursued you:
Silence, the desk, the flippant expression, the night, the
 accustomed routine, — if these conceal you from
 others, or from yourself, they do not conceal you
 from me.
The shaved face, the unsteady eye, the impure complexion, — if these balk others, they do not balk me.
The pert apparel, the deformed attitude, drunkenness,
 greed, premature death, — all these I part aside.
I track through your windings and turnings, — I come
 upon you where you thought eye should never
 come upon you."

Whitman said, in the now famous preface of 1855, that "the greatest poet does not moralize, or make applications of morals, — he knows the soul." There is no preaching or reproof in the "Leaves."

HIS RELATION TO LIFE

"I sit and look out upon all the sorrows of the world, and
     upon all oppression and shame;
I hear secret convulsive sobs from young men, at anguish
     with themselves, remorseful after deeds done;
I see, in low life, the mother misused by her children,
     dying, neglected, gaunt, desperate;
I see the wife misused by her husband; I see the treach-
     erous seducer of the young woman;
I mark the ranklings of jealousy and unrequited love, at-
     tempted to be hid, — I see these sights on the earth,
I see the workings of battle, pestilence, tyranny; I see
     martyrs and prisoners,
I observe a famine at sea, — I observe the sailors casting
     lots who shall be killed, to preserve the lives of the
     rest,
I observe the slights and degradations cast by arrogant
     persons upon laborers, the poor, and upon ne-
     groes, and the like;
All these — all the meanness and agony without end I
     sitting look out upon,
See, hear, and am silent."

Only once does he shame and rebuke the offender;
then he holds up to him " a hand-mirror."

"Hold it up sternly! See this it sends back! (who is it? is
     it you?)
Outside fair costume, — within, ashes and filth.
No more a flashing eye, — no more a sonorous voice or
     springy step,
Now some slave's eye, voice, hands, step,

A drunkard's breath, unwholesome eater's face, vene-
    realee's flesh,
Lungs rotting away piecemeal, stomach sour and canker-
    ous,
Joints rheumatic, bowels clogged with abomination,
Blood circulating dark and poisonous streams,
Words babble, hearing and touch callous,
No brain, no heart left, no magnetism of sex;
Such, from one look in this looking-glass ere you go hence,
Such a result so soon — and from such a beginning!''

The poet's way is so different from the moralist's
way! The poet confesses all, loves all, — has no
preferences. He is moral only in his results. We ask
ourselves, Does he breathe the air of health? Can
he stand the test of nature? Is he tonic and inspir-
ing? That he shocks us is nothing. The first touch
of the sea is a shock. Does he toughen us, does he
help make arterial blood?

All that men do and are guilty of attracts him.
Their vices and excesses, — he would make these
his own also. He is jealous lest he be thought better
than other men, — lest he seem to stand apart from
even criminals and offenders. When the passion for
human brotherhood is upon him, he is balked by nothing; he goes down into the social mire to find his
lovers and equals. In the pride of our morality and
civic well-being, this phase of his work shocks us;
but there are moods when the soul says it is good,
and we rejoice in the strong man that can do it.

The restrictions, denials, and safeguards put upon us by the social order, and the dictates of worldly prudence, fall only before a still more fervid human-ism, or a still more vehement love.

The vital question is, Where does he leave us? On firmer ground, or in the mire? Depleted and enervated, or full and joyous? In the gloom of pessimism, or in the sunlight of its opposite? —

"*So long !*
I announce a man or woman coming — perhaps you are
    the one;
I announce a great individual, fluid as Nature, chaste,
    affectionate, compassionate, fully armed.

"*So long !*
I announce a life that shall be copious, vehement, spirit-
    ual, bold,
And I announce an old age that shall lightly and joyfully
    meet its translation.

"I announce myriads of youths, beautiful, gigantic, sweet-
    blooded;
I announce a race of splendid and savage old men."

There is no contradiction here. The poet sounds all the experiences of life, and he gives out the true note at last.

"No specification is necessary, — all that a male or fe-
    male does, that is vigorous, benevolent, clean, is so

much profit to him or her, in the unshakable order of the universe, and through the whole scope of it forever."

VIII

Nothing but the most uncompromising religious purpose can justify certain things in the "Leaves;" nothing but the most buoyant and pervasive spirituality can justify its overwhelming materiality; nothing but the most creative imagination can offset its tremendous realism; nothing but the note of universal brotherhood can atone for its vehement Americanism; nothing but the primal spirit of poesy itself can make amends for this open flouting of the routine poetic, and this endless procession before us of the common and the familiar.

IX

Whitman loved the word "unrefined." It was one of the words he would have us apply to himself. He was unrefined, as the air, the soil, the water, and all sweet natural things are unrefined (fine but not *re*fined). He applies the word to himself two or three times in the course of his poems. He loved the words sun-tan, air-sweetness, brawn, etc. He speaks of his "savage song," not to call forth the bards of the past, he says, but to invoke the bards of the future.

"Have I sung so capricious and loud my savage songs?"

The thought that his poems might help contribute to the production of a "race of splendid and savage old men" was dear to him. He feared the depleting and emasculating effects of our culture and conventions. The decay of maternity and paternity in this country, the falling off of the native populations, were facts full of evil omen. His ideal of manly or womanly character is rich in all the purely human qualities and attributes; rich in sex, in sympathy, in temperament; physiologically sound and clean, as well as mentally and morally so.

"Fear grace, fear delicatesse;
Fear the mellow-sweet, the sucking of honey-juice:
Beware the advancing mortal ripening of nature!
Beware what precedes the decay of the ruggedness of
    states and men."

He was himself the savage old man he invoked. It was no part of his plan to preach, in refined and euphonious terms, hygiene and the value of the natural man, but to project into literature the thing itself, to exploit a character coarse as well as fine, and to imbue his poems with a physiological quality as well as a psychological and intellectual.

" I will scatter the new roughness and gladness among
    them."

He says to the pale, impotent victim of over-refinement, with intentional rudeness,

"Open your scarf'd chops till I blow grit within you."

X

One of the key-words to Whitman both as a man and a poet is the word "composite." He was probably the most composite man this century has produced, and in this respect at least is representative of the American of the future, who must be the result of the blending of more diverse racial elements than any man of history. He seems to have had an intuition of his composite character when he said in his first poem: —

"I am large, — I contain multitudes."

The London correspondent of the "New York Tribune," in reluctantly conceding at the time of the poet's death something to the British admiration of him, said he was "rich in temperament." The phrase is well chosen. An English expert on the subject of temperament, who visited Whitman some years ago, said he had all four temperaments, the sanguine, the nervous, the melancholic, and the lymphatic, while most persons have but two temperaments, and rarely three.

It was probably the composite character of Whitman that caused him to attract such diverse and opposite types of men, — scholars and workingmen, lawyers, doctors, scientists, and men of the world, — and that made him personally such a puzzle to most people, — so impossible to classify. On the street the promenaders would turn and look after him, and I have often heard them ask each other, " What man was that ? " He has often been taken for a doctor, and during his services in the army hospitals various myths were floating about concerning him. Now he was a benevolent Catholic priest, — then some unknown army general, or retired sea captain; at one time he was reputed to be one of the owners of the Cunard line of steamers. To be. taken for a Californian was common. One recalls the composite character of the poet whom he outlines in his poems (see quotation, page 181).

The book is as composite as the man. It is all things to all men; it lends itself to a multitude of interpretations. Every earnest reader of it will find some clew or suggestion by the aid of which he fancies he can unlock the whole book, but in the end he will be pretty sure to discover that one key is not enough. To one critic, his book is the " hoarse song of a man," its manly and masculine element attracts him; to another he is the poet of joy, to another the poet of health, to still another he is the bard of personality; others read him as the poet of nature, or the poet of democracy. His French critic, Gabriel Sarrazin, calls him an apostle, — the apostle of the idea that man is an indivisible fragment of the universal Divinity.

XI

What has a poet of Whitman's aim to do with decency or indecency, with modesty or immodesty? These are social or conventional virtues; he represents mainly primary qualities and forces. Does life, does death, does nature, respect our proprieties, our conventional veils and illusions? Neither will he. He will strip them all away. He will act and speak as if all things in the universe were equally sacred and divine; as if all men were really his brothers, all women his sisters; as if all parts of the human body were equally beautiful and wonderful; as if fatherhood and motherhood, birth and begetting, were sacred acts. Of course it is easy to see that this course will speedily bring him in collision with the guardians of taste and social morality. But what of that? He professes to take his cue from the elemental laws. "I reckon I behave no more proudly than the level I plant my house by." The question is, Is he adequate, is he man enough, to do it? Will he not falter, or betray self-consciousness? Will he be true to his ideal through thick and thin? The social gods will all be outraged, but that is less to him than the candor and directness of nature in whose spirit he assumes to speak.

Nothing is easier than to convict Walt Whitman

of what is called indecency; he laughs indifferent
when you have done so. It is not your gods that
he serves. He says he would be as indifferent of
observation as the trees or rocks. And it is here that
we must look for his justification, upon ethical rather
than upon the grounds of conventional art. He
has taken our sins upon himself. He has applied
to the morbid sex-consciousness, that has eaten so
deeply into our social system, the heroic treatment;
he has fairly turned it naked into the street. He has
not merely in words denied the inherent vileness of
sex; he has denied it in very deed. We should not
have taken offense had he confined himself to words,
— had he said sex is pure, the body is as clean about
the loins as about the head; but being an artist, a
creator, and not a mere thinker or preacher, he was
compelled to act, — to do the thing instead of saying it.

The same in other matters. Being an artist, he
could not merely say all men were his brothers; he
must show them as such. If their weakness and
sins are his also, he must not flinch when it comes
to the test; he must make his words good. We may
be shocked at the fullness and minuteness of the
specification, but that is no concern of his; he deals
with the concrete and not with the abstract, —
fraternity and equality as a reality, not as a sentiment.

XII

In the phase in which we are now considering him, Whitman appears as the Adamic man re-born here in the nineteenth century, or with science and the modern added, and fully and fearlessly embodying himself in a poem. It is stronger than we can stand, but it is good for us, and one of these days, or one of these centuries, we shall be able to stand it and enjoy it.

"To the garden the world anew ascending,
Potent mates, daughters, sons, preluding,
The love, the life of their bodies, meaning and being,
Curious, here behold my resurrection, after slumber,
The revolving cycles, in their wide sweep, having brought
    me again,
Amorous, mature — all beautiful to me — all wondrous,
My limbs, and the quivering fire that ever plays through
    them, for reasons most wondrous;
Existing, I peer and penetrate still,
Content with the present — content with the past,
By my side, or back of me, Eve following,
Or in front, and I following her just the same."

The critics perpetually misread Whitman because they fail to see this essentially composite and dramatic character of his work, — that it is not the song of Walt Whitman the private individual, but of Walt Whitman as representative of, and speaking

for, all types and conditions of men; in fact, that
it is the drama of a new democratic personality, a
character outlined on a larger, more copious, more
vehement scale than has yet appeared in the world.
The germs of this character he would sow broadcast
over the land.

In this drama of personality the poet always
identifies himself with the scene, incident, experience, or person he delineates, or for whom he
speaks. He says to the New Englander, or to the
man of the South and the West, "I depict you as
myself." In the same way he depicts offenders,
roughs, criminals, and low and despised persons as
himself; he lays claim to every sin of omission and
commission men are guilty of, because, he says,
"the germs are in all men." Men dare not tell their
faults. He will make them all his own, and then tell
them; there shall be full confession for once.

"If you become degraded, criminal, ill, then I become so
      for your sake;
If you remember your foolish and outlaw'd deeds, do you
      think I cannot remember my own foolish and out-
      law'd deeds?"

It will not do to read this poet, or any great poet,
in a narrow and exacting spirit. As Whitman himself says: "The messages of great poems to each
man and woman are: Come to us on equal terms,
only then can you understand us."

217

In the much misunderstood group of poems called
"Children of Adam" the poet speaks for the male
generative principle, and all the excesses and abuses
that grow out of it he unblushingly imputes to himself. What men have done and still do, while under
the intoxication of the sexual passion, he does, he
makes it all his own experience.

That we have here a revelation of his own personal taste and experiences may or may not be the
case, but we have no more right to assume it than
we have to assume that all other poets speak from
experience when they use the first person singular.
When John Brown mounted the scaffold in Virginia, in 1860, the poet says: —

"I was at hand, silent I stood with teeth shut close, I
  watch'd,
I stood very near you, old man, when cool and indifferent,
   but trembling with age and your unheal'd wounds,
   you mounted the scaffold," —

very near him he stood in spirit; very near him he
stood in the person of others, but not in his own
proper person.

If we take this poet literally, we shall believe he
has been in California and Oregon; that he has set
foot in every city on the continent; that he grew
up in Virginia; that every Southern State has been
by turns his home; that he has been a soldier, a
sailor, a miner; that he has lived in Dakota's woods,

his "diet meat, his drink from the spring;" that he
has lived on the plains with hunters and ranchmen,
etc. He lays claim to all these characters, all these
experiences, because what others do, what others
assume, or suffer, or enjoy, that he appropriates to
himself.

"I am the hounded slave, I wince at the bite of the dogs,
Hell and despair are upon me, crack and again crack the
      marksmen,
I clutch the rails of the fence, my gore dribs, thinned with
      the ooze of my skin,
I fall on the weeds and stones,
The riders spur their unwilling horses, haul close,
Taunt my dizzy ears, and beat me violently over the head
      with whipstocks.

"Agonies are one of my changes of garments,
I do not ask the wounded person how he feels — I myself
      become the wounded person,
My hurts turn livid upon me as I lean on a cane and
      observe.

"I become any presence or truth of humanity here,
See myself in prison shaped like another man,
And feel the dull unintermitted pain.

"For me the keepers of convicts shoulder their carbines
      and keep watch,
It is I let out in the morning and barred at night.
Not a mutineer walks handcuffed to the jail, but I am
      handcuffed to him and walk by his side."

XIII

It is charged against Whitman that he does not celebrate love at all, and very justly. He had no purpose to celebrate the sentiment of love. Literature is vastly overloaded with this element already. He celebrates fatherhood and motherhood, and the need of well-begotten, physiologically well-begotten offspring. Of that veiled prurient suggestion which readers so delight in — of "bosoms mutinously fair," and "the soul-lingering loops of perfumed hair," as one of our latest poets puts it — there is no hint in his volume. He would have fallen from grace the moment he had attempted such a thing. Any trifling or dalliance on his part would have been his ruin. Love as a sentiment has fairly run riot in literature. From Whitman's point of view, it would have been positively immoral for him either to have vied with the lascivious poets in painting it as the forbidden, or with the sentimental poets in depicting it as a charm. Woman with him is always the mate and equal of the man, never his plaything,

Whitman is seldom or never the poet of a sentiment, at least of the domestic and social sentiments. His is more the voice of the eternal, abysmal man.

The home, the fireside, the domestic allurements, are not in him; love, as we find it in other poets, is not in him; the idyllic, except in touches here and there, is not in him; the choice, the finished, the perfumed, the romantic, the charm of art and the delight of form, are not to be looked for in his pages. The cosmic takes the place of the idyllic; the begetter, the Adamic man, takes the place of the lover; patriotism takes the place of family affection; charity takes the place of piety; love of kind is more than love of neighbor; the poet and the artist are swallowed up in the seer and the prophet.

The poet evidently aimed to put in his sex poems a rank and healthful animality, and to make them as frank as the shedding of pollen by the trees, strong even to the point of offense. He could not make it pleasing, a sweet morsel to be rolled under the tongue; that would have been levity and sin, as in Byron and the other poets. It must be direct and rank, healthfully so. The courage that did it, and showed no wavering of self-consciousness, was more than human. Man is a begetter. How shall a poet in our day and land treat this fact? With levity and by throwing over it the lure of the forbidden, the attraction of the erotic? That is one way, the way of nearly all the poets of the past. But that is not Whitman's way. He would sooner be bestial than Byronic, he would sooner shock by his frankness than inflame by his suggestion. And this in the interest of health and longevity, not in the interest of a prurient and effeminate "art." In these poems Whitman for a moment emphasizes sex, the need of sex, and the power of sex. "All were

221

lacking if sex were lacking." He says to men and women, Here is where you live after all, here is the seat of empire. You are at the top of your condition when you are fullest and sanest there. Fearful consequences follow any corrupting or abusing or perverting of sex. The poet stands in the garden of the world naked and not ashamed. It is a great comfort that he could do it in this age of hectic lust and Swinburnian impotence, — that he could do it and not be ridiculous. To have done it without offense would have been proof that he had failed utterly. Let us be shocked; it is a wholesome shock, like the douse of the sea, or the buffet of the wind. We shall be all the better for it by and by.

XIV

The lover of Whitman comes inevitably to associate him with character and personal qualities. I sometimes meet women whom I say are of the Whitman type — the kind of woman he invoked and predicted. They bear children, and are not ashamed; motherhood is their pride and their joy: they are cheerful, tolerant, friendly, think no evil, meet high and low on equal terms; they walk, row, climb mountains; they reach forth into the actual world of questions and events, open-minded, sympathetic, frank, natural, good-natured; the mates and companions of their husbands, keeping pace with them in all matters; home-makers, but larger than home, considerate, forgiving, unceremonious, — in short, the large, fresh, wholesome open-air natures whose ideal so completely possessed Walt Whitman.

A British critic wisely says the gift of Whitman to us is the gift of life rather than of literature, but it is the gift of life through literature. Indeed, Whitman means a life as much as Christianity means a life. He says: —

> "Writing and talk do not prove me."

Nothing but the test of reality finally proves him: —

> "The proof of the poet shall be sternly deferr'd till his country has absorbed him as affectionately as he has absorbed it."

The proof of Whitman shall be deferred till he has borne fruit in actual, concrete life.

He knew that merely intellectual and artistic tests did not settle matters in his case, or that we would not reach his final value by making a dead-set at him through the purely æsthetic faculties. Is he animating to life itself? Can we absorb and assimilate him? Does he nourish the manly and heroic virtues? Does he make us more religious, more tolerant, more charitable, more candid, more self-reliant? If not, he fails of his chief end. It is doubtful if the purely scholarly and literary poets, like Milton, say, or like our own Poe, are ever absorbed in the sense above implied; while there is little doubt that poets like Homer, like Shakespeare, are absorbed and modify a people's manners and ideals. Only that which we love affects our lives. Our admiration for art and literature as such is something entirely outside the sources of character and power of action.

Whitman identifies himself with our lives. We associate him with reality, with days, scenes, persons, events. The youth who reads Poe or Lowell wants to be a scholar, a wit, a poet, a writer; the youth who reads Whitman wants to be a man, and to get at the meaning and value of life. Our author's bent towards real things, real men and women, and his power to feed and foster personality, are unmistakable.

Life, reality, alone proves him; a saner and more robust fatherhood and motherhood, more practical democracy, more charity, more love, more comradeship, more social equality, more robust ideals of womanly and manly character, prove him. When we are more tolerant and patient and long-suffering, when the strain of our worldly, commercial spirit relaxes, then is he justified. Whitman means a letting-up of the strain all along the line, — less hurry, less greed, less rivalry, more leisure, more charity, more fraternalism and altruism, more religion, less formality and convention.

"When America does what was promised,
    When each part is peopled with free people,

When there is no city on earth to lead my city, the city of
      young men, the Mannahatta city — but when the
      Mannahatta leads all the cities of the earth,

When there are plentiful athletic bards, inland and sea-
      board,

When through these States walk a hundred millions of
      superb persons,

When the rest part away for superb persons, and contrib-
      ute to them,

When fathers, firm, unconstrained, open-eyed — when
      breeds of the most perfect mothers denote America,

Then to me ripeness and conclusion."

XV

After all, I think it matters little whether we call
him poet or not. Grant that he is not a poet in the
usual or technical sense, but poet-prophet, or poet-
seer, or all combined. He is a poet plus something
else. It is when he is judged less than poet, or no
poet at all, that we feel injustice is done him. Grant
that his work is not art, that it does not give off
the perfume, the atmosphere of the highly wrought
artistic works like those of Tennyson, but of something quite different.

We have all been slow to see that his cherished
ends were religious rather than literary; that, over
and above all else, he was a great religious teacher
and prophet. Had he been strictly a literary poet,
like Lowell, or Longfellow, or Tennyson, — that

is, a writer working for purely artistic effects, — we should be compelled to judge him quite differently.

"Leaves of Grass" is a gospel — glad tidings of great joy to those who are prepared to receive it. Its final value lies in its direct, intense, personal appeal; in what it did for Symonds, who said it made a man of him; in what it did for Stevenson, who said it dispelled a thousand illusions; in what it did for Mrs. Gilchrist, who said it enabled her to find her own soul; in what it does for all earnest readers of it in blending with the inmost current of their lives. Whitman is the life-giver of our time. How shall a poet give us life but by making us share his larger measure of life, his larger hope, his larger love, his larger charity, his saner and wider outlook? What are the three great life-giving principles? Can we name them better than St. Paul named them eighteen hundred years ago, — faith, hope, charity? And these are the cornerstones of Whitman's work, — a faith so broad and fervent that it accepts death as joyously as life, and sees all things at last issue in spiritual results; a hope that sees the golden age ahead of us, not behind us; and a charity that balks at nothing, that makes him identify himself with offenders and outlaws; a charity as great as his who said to the thief on the cross, "This day thou shalt be with me in paradise."

To cry up faith, hope, and charity is not to make men partakers of them; but to exemplify them in a survey of the whole problem of life, to make them vital as hearing or eyesight in a work of the imagination, to show them as motives and impulses controlling all the rest, is to beget and foster them in the mind of the beholder.

He is more and he is less than the best of the other poets. The popular, the conventional poets are mainly occupied with the artistic side of things, — with that which refines, solaces, beautifies. Whitman is mainly occupied with the cosmic and universal side of things, and the human and spiritual values that may be extracted from them. His poetry is not the result of the same kind of selection and partiality as that we are more familiar with.

Hence, while the message of Tennyson and his kind is the message of beauty, the message of Whitman is, in a much fuller sense, the message of life. He speaks the word of faith and power. This is his distinction; he is the life-giver. Such a man comes that we may have life, and have it more abundantly.

The message of beauty, — who would undervalue it? The least poet and poetling lisps some word or syllable of it. The masters build its temples and holy places. All own it, all receive it gladly. But the gospel of life, there is danger that we shall not know it when we hear it. It is a harsher and more heroic strain than the other. It calls no man to his ease, or to be lulled and soothed. It is a summons and a challenge. It lays rude, strong hands upon you. It filters and fibres your blood. It is more of the frost, the rains, the winds, than of cushions or parlors.

The call of life is a call to battle always. We are stronger by the strength of every obstacle or enemy overcome.

"Listen! I will be honest with you,
I do not offer the old smooth prizes, but offer rough new prizes,
These are the days that must happen to you:

"You shall not heap up what is called riches,
You shall scatter with lavish hand all that you earn or achieve;
You but arrive at the city to which you were destined — you hardly settle yourself to satisfaction, before you are called by an irresistible call to depart.
You shall be treated to the ironical smiles and mockings of those who remain behind you;
What beckonings of love you receive, you shall only answer with passionate kisses of parting,
You shall not allow the hold of those who spread their reached hands toward you.

"Allons! After the GREAT COMPANIONS! and to belong to them!"

HIS RELATION TO LIFE

XVI

Whitman always avails himself of the poet's privilege and magnifies himself. He magnifies others in the same ratio, he magnifies all things. "Magnifying and applying come I," he says, "outbidding at the start the old cautious hucksters." Indeed, the character which speaks throughout "Leaves of Grass" is raised to the highest degree of personal exaltation. To it nothing is trivial, nothing is mean; all is good, all is divine. The usual distinctions disappear, burned up, the poet says, for religion's sake. All the human attributes are heightened and enlarged; sympathy as wide as the world; love that balks at nothing; charity as embracing as the sky; egotism like the force of gravity; religious fervor that consumes the coarsest facts like stubble; spirituality that finds God everywhere every hour of the day; faith that welcomes death as cheerfully as life; comradeship that would weld the nation into a family of brothers; sexuality that makes prudes shudder; poetic enthusiasm that scornfully dispenses with all the usual adventitious aids; and in general a largeness, coarseness, and vehemence that are quite appalling to the general reader. Lovers of poetry will of necessity be very slow in adjusting their notions to the standards of "Leaves of Grass." It is a survey of life and of the world from the cosmic rather than from the conventional standpoint. It carries the standards of the natural universal into all fields.

Some men have accepted poverty and privation with such contentment and composure as to make us almost envious of their lot; and Whitman accepts the coarser, commoner human elements which he finds in himself, and which most of us try to conceal or belittle, with such frankness and perception of their real worth that they acquire new meaning and value in our eyes. If he paraded these things unduly, and showed an overweening preference for them, as some of his critics charge, this is of course an element of weakness.

His precept and his illustration, carried out in life, would fill the land with strong, native, original types of men and women animated by the most vehement comradeship, selfism and otherism going hand in hand.

HIS RELATION TO CULTURE

I

"LEAVES OF GRASS" is not the poetry of culture, but it is to be said in the same breath that it is not such a work as an uncultured man produces, or is capable of producing.

The uncultured man does not think Whitman's thoughts, or propose Whitman's problems to himself, or understand or appreciate them at all. The "Leaves" are perhaps of supreme interest only to men of deepest culture, because they contain in such ample measure that without which all culture is mere varnish or veneer. They are indirectly a tremendous criticism of American life and civilization, and they imply that breadth of view and that liberation of spirit — that complete disillusioning — which is the best result of culture, and which all great souls have reached, no matter who or what their schoolmasters may have been.

Our reading public probably does not and cannot see itself in Whitman at all. He must be a great shock to its sense of the genteel and the respectable. Nor can the working people and the unlettered, though they were drawn to Whitman the man, be expected to respond to any considerable extent to

Whitman the poet. His standpoint can be reached only after passing through many things and freeing one's self from many illusions. He is more representative of the time-spirit out of which America grew, and which is now shaping the destiny of the race upon this continent. He strikes under and through our whole civilization.

He despised our social gods, he distrusted our book-culture, he was alarmed at the tendency to the depletion and attenuation of the national type, and he aimed to sow broadcast the germs of more manly ideals. His purpose was to launch his criticism from the basic facts of human life, psychic and physiologic; to inject into the veins of our anæmic literature the reddest, healthiest kind of blood; and in doing so he has given free swing to the primary human traits and affections and to sexuality, and has charged his pages with the spirit of real things, real life.

We have been so long used to verse which is the outcome of the literary impulse alone, which is written at so many removes from the primary human qualities, produced from the extreme verge of culture and artificial refinement, which is so innocent of the raciness and healthful coarseness of nature, that poetry which has these qualities, which implies the body as well as the mind, which is the direct outgrowth of a radical human personality, and which make demands like those made by real things, is either an offense to us or is misunderstood.

II

Whitman says his book is not a good lesson, but it takes down the bars to a good lesson, and that to another, and that to another still. To take down bars rather than to put them up is always Whitman's aim; to make his reader free of the universe, to turn him forth into the fresh and inexhaustible pastures of time, space, eternity, and with a smart slap upon his back with the halter as a spur and send-off, is about what he would do. His message, first and last, is "give play to yourself;" "let yourself go;" — happiness is in the quest of happiness; power comes to him who power uses.

"Long enough have you timidly waded, holding a plank
        by the shore;
  Now I will you to be a bold swimmer,
  To jump off in the midst of the sea, rise again, nod to
        me, shout, and laughingly dash with your hair."

To hold Whitman up to ridicule, and to convict him of grossness and tediousness, is easy enough; first, because he is so out of relation to the modes and tastes of his times, and, secondly, because he has somewhat of the uncouthness and coarseness of large bodies. Then his seriousness and simplicity, like that of Biblical and Oriental writers, — a kind of childish inaptness and homeliness, — often exposes him to our keen, almost abnormal sense of the ridiculous. He was deficient in humor, and he wrote his book in entire obliviousness of social usages and conventions, so that the perspective of it is not the social or indoor perspective, but that of life and nature at large, careering and unhampered. It is probably the one modern poem whose standards are not social and what are called artistic.

Its atmosphere is always that of the large, free spaces of vast, unhoused nature. It has been said that the modern world could be reconstructed from "Leaves of Grass," so compendious and all-inclusive is it in its details; but of the modern world as a social organization, of man as the creature of social usages and prohibitions, of fashions, of dress, of ceremony, — the indoor, parlor and drawing-room man, — there is no hint in its pages. In its matter and in its spirit, in its standards and in its execution, in its ideals and in its processes, it belongs to and affiliates with open-air nature, often reaching, I think, the cosmic and unconditioned. In a new sense is Whitman the brother of the orbs and cosmic processes, "conveying a sentiment and invitation of the earth." All his enthusiasms, all his sympathies have to do with the major and fundamental elements of life. He is a world-poet. We do not readily adjust our indoor notions to him. Our culture-standards do not fit him.

The problem of the poet is doubtless more difficult in our day than in any past day; it is harder
for him to touch reality.

The accumulations of our civilization are enormous: an artificial world of great depth and potency
overlies the world of reality; especially does it over-
lie the world of man's moral and intellectual nature.
Most of us live and thrive in this artificial world,
and never know but it is the world of God's own
creating. Only now and then a man strikes his
roots down through this made land into fresh, virgin soil. When the religious genius strikes his roots
through it, and insists upon a present revelation,
we are apt to cry "heretic;" when the poet strikes
his roots through it, as Whitman did, and insists
upon giving us reality, — giving us himself before
custom or law, — we cry "barbarian," or "art-
heretic," or "outlaw of art."

In the countless adjustments and accumulations,
and in the oceanic currents of our day and land, the
individual is more and more lost sight of, — merged,
swamped, effaced. See him in Whitman rising
above it all. See it all shot through and through
with his quality and obedient to his will. See the
all-leveling tendency of democracy, the effacing and
sterilizing power of a mechanical and industrial
age, set at naught or reversed by a single towering

personality. See America, its people, their doings, their types, their good and evil traits, all bodied forth in one composite character, and this character justifying itself and fronting the universe with the old joy and contentment.

IV

"The friendly and flowing savage, who is he?
Is he waiting for civilization, or is he past it and
master of it?"

Do we not, consciously or unconsciously, ask this or a similar question of every poet or artist whom we pass in review before us? Is he master of his culture, or does it master him? Does he strike back through it to simple, original nature, or is he a potted plant? Does he retain the native savage virtues, or is he entirely built up from the outside? We constantly mistake culture for mere refinement, which it is not: it is a liberating process; it is a clearing away of obstructions, and the giving to inherent virtues a chance to express themselves. It makes savage nature friendly and considerate. The aim of culture is not to get rid of nature, but to utilize nature. The great poet is always a "friendly and flowing savage," the master and never the slave of the complex elements of our artificial lives.

Though our progress and civilization are a triumph over nature, yet in an important sense we never get away from nature or improve upon her.

Her standards are still our standards, her sweetness and excellence are still our aim. Her health, her fertility, her wholeness, her freshness, her innocence, her evolution, we would fain copy or reproduce. We would, if we could, keep the pungency and aroma of her wild fruit in our cultivated specimens, the virtue and hardiness of the savage in our fine gentlemen, the joy and spontaneity of her bird-songs in our poetry, the grace and beauty of her forms in our sculpture and carvings.

A poetic utterance from an original, individual standpoint, something definite and characteristic, — this is always the crying need. What a fine talent has this or that young British or American poet whom we might name! But we see that the singer has not yet made this talent his own; it is a kind of borrowed capital; it is the general taste and intelligence that speak. When will he redeem all these promises, and become a fixed centre of thought and emotion in himself? To write poems is no distinction; to be a poem, to be a fixed point amid the seething chaos, a rock amid the currents, giving your own form and character to them, — that is something.

It matters little, as Whitman himself says, who contributes the mass of poetic verbiage upon which any given age feeds.

But for a national first-class poem, or a great work of the imagination of any sort, the man is everything, because such works finally rest upon primary human qualities and special individual traits. A richly endowed personality is always the main dependence in such cases, or, as Goethe says, "in the great work the great person is always present as the great factor."

"Leaves of Grass" is as distinctly an emanation from Walt Whitman, from his quality and equipment as a man apart from anything he owed to books or to secondary influences, as a tree is an emanation from the soil. It is, moreover, an emanation from him as an American in the latter half of the nineteenth century, and as a typical democratic composite man, a man of the common people, bone of their bone and flesh of their flesh, but with an extraordinary endowment of spiritual and intellectual power, to which he has given full swing without abating one jot or tittle the influence of his heritage of the common stock.

v

There is one important quality that enters into all first-class literary production and into all art, which is taken little account of in current criticism: I mean the quality of the manly, — the pulse and pressure of manly virility and strength. Goethe spoke of it to Eckermann as a certain urgent power in which the art of his time was lacking. The producers had taste and skill, but were not masterful as men. Goethe always looked straight through the work to the man behind it; in art and poetry the personality was everything. The special talent of one kind or another was quite secondary. The greatest works are the least literary. To speak in literature as a man, and not merely as a scholar or professional littérateur, is always the crying need. The new poet has this or that gift, but what is the human fund back of all? What is his endowment of the common universal human traits? How much of a man is he? His measure in this respect will be the measure of the final value of his contribution.

The decadence of literature sets in when there is more talent than character in current production; when rare literary and artistic gifts no longer come wedded to large human and manly gifts; when taste is fastidious rather than robust and hearty. When was there a man born to English or American literature with a large endowment of the universal human qualities, or with those elements that give breadth and power, and which lead art rather than follow it? We are living in an age of great purity and refinement of taste in art and letters, but destitute of power. Goethe spoke of Walter Scott not merely as a great talent, but as a "comprehensive nature." Without this comprehensive nature as a setting, his great talent would have amounted to but little. This gives the weight, the final authority. How little there was on the surface of Scott of the literary keenness, subtlety, knowingness of later producers, and yet how far his contribution surpasses theirs in real human pathos and suggestiveness!

The same might be said of Count Tolstoï, who is also, back of all, a great loving nature.

One has great joy in Whitman because he is beyond and over all a large and loving personality; his work is but a thin veil through which a great nature clearly shows. The urgent power of which Goethe speaks is almost too strong, — too strong for current taste: we want more art and less man, more literature and less life. It is not merely a great mind that we feel, but a great character. It penetrates every line, and indeed makes it true of the book that whoever "touches this touches a man."

The lesson of the poet is all in the direction of the practical manly and womanly qualities and virtues, — health, temperance, sanity, power, endurance, aplomb, — and not at all in the direction of the literary and artistic qualities or culture.

"To stand the cold or heat, to take good aim with a gun, to sail a boat, to manage horses, to beget superb children,

To speak readily and clearly, to feel at home among common people,

To hold our own in terrible positions on land and sea."

All his aims, ideas, impulses, aspirations, relate to life, to personality, and to power to deal with real things; and if we expect from him only literary ideas, — form, beauty, lucidity, proportion, — we shall be disappointed. He seeks to make the impression of concrete forces and objects, and not of art.

"Not for an embroiderer
(There will always be plenty of embroiderers, — I welcome them also),
But for the fibre of things, and for inherent men and women.

"Not to chisel ornaments,
But to chisel with free stroke the heads and limbs of plenteous Supreme Gods, that The States may realize them, walking and talking."

His whole work is a radiation from an exemplification of the idea that there is something better than to be an artist or a poet, — namely, to be a man. The poet's rapture springs not merely from the contemplation of the beautiful and the artistic, but from the contemplation of the whole; from the contemplation of democracy, the common people, workingmen, soldiers, sailors, his own body, death, sex, manly love, occupations, and the force and vitality of things. We are to look for the clues to him in the open air and in natural products, rather than in the traditional art forms and methods. He

declares he will never again mention love or death
inside of a house, and that he will translate himself
only to those who privately stay with him in the
open air.

"If you would understand me, go to the heights or water-
shore;
The nearest gnat is an explanation, and a drop or
motion of waves a key:
The maul, the oar, the handsaw, second my words.

"No shuttered room or school can commune with me,
But roughs and little children better than they.

"The young mechanic is closest to me — he knows me
pretty well.
The woodman, that takes his axe and jug with him,
shall take me with him all day;
The farm-boy, ploughing in the field, feels good at
the sound of my voice:
In vessels that sail, my words sail — I go with fisher-
men and seamen, and love them.

"My face rubs to the hunter's face when he lies down
alone in his blanket;
The driver, thinking of me, does not mind the jolt of
his wagon;
The young mother and old mother comprehend me;
The girl and the wife rest the needle a moment, and
forget where they are:
They and all would resume what I have told them."

VI

So far as literature is a luxury, and for the cultured, privileged few, its interests are not in Whitman; so far as poetry represents the weakness of
man rather than his strength; so far as it expresses a
shrinking from reality and a refuge in sentimentalism; so far as it is aristocratic as in Tennyson, or
mocking and rebellious as in Byron, or erotic and
mephitic as in Swinburne, or regretful and remini-
scent as in Arnold, or a melodious baying of the
moon as in Shelley, or the outcome of mere scholarly
and technical acquirements as in so many of our
younger poets, — so far as literature or poetry, I
say, stand for these things, there is little of either
in Whitman. Whitman stands for the primary and
essential; he stands for that which makes the body
as well as the mind, which makes life sane and joyous and masterful. Everything that tends to depletion, satiety, the abnormal, the erotic and exotic,
that induces the stress and fever of life, is foreign to
his spirit. He is less beautiful than the popular
poets, yet more beautiful. He will have to do only
with the inevitable beauty, the beauty that comes
unsought, that resides in the interior meanings and
affiliations, — the beauty that dare turn its back
upon the beautiful.

Whitman has escaped entirely the literary disease, the characteristic symptom of which, accord-

ing to Renan, is that people love less things themselves than the literary effects which they produce.
He has escaped the art disease, which makes art all
in all; the religious disease, which runs to maudlin
piety and seeks to win heaven by denying earth;
the beauty disease, which would make of poesy
a conventional flower-garden. He brings heroic
remedies for our morbid sex-consciousness, and for
all the pathological conditions brought about by
our excess of refinement, and the dyspeptic deple-
tions of our indoor, artificial lives. Whitman with-
stood the æsthetic temptation, as Amiel calls it, to
which most of our poets fall a victim, — the lust for
the merely beautiful, the epicureanism of the literary faculties. We can make little of him if we are
in quest of æsthetic pleasures alone. "In order to
establish those literary authorities which are called
classic centuries," says Renan, "something healthy
and solid is necessary. Common household bread
is of more value here than pastry." But the vast
majority of literary producers aim at pastry, or,
worse yet, confectionery, — something especially
delightful and titivating to the taste. No doubt
Renan himself was something of a literary epicure,
but then he imposed upon himself large and serious
tasks, and his work as a whole is solid and nour-
ishing; his charm of style does not blind and seduce
us. It makes all the difference in the world whether
we seek the beautiful through the true, or the true

through the beautiful. Seek ye the kingdom of
truth first, and all things shall be added. The
novice aims to write beautifully, but the master aims
to see truly and to feel vitally. Beauty follows him,
and is never followed by him.

Nature is beautiful because she is something else
first, yes, and last, too, and all the while. Whitman's
work is baptized in the spirit of the whole, and its
health and sweetness in this respect, when compared
with the over-refined artistic works, is like that of
a laborer in the fields compared with the pale, dyspeptic ennuyé.

VII

Whitman's ideal is undoubtedly much larger,
coarser, stronger — much more racy and democratic
— than the ideal we are familiar with in current
literature, and upon which our culture is largely
based. He applies the democratic spirit not only
to the material of poetry, — excluding all the old
stock themes of love and war, lords and ladies,
myths and fairies and legends, — but he applies it
to the form as well, excluding rhyme and measure
and all the conventional verse architecture. His
work stands or it falls upon its inherent, its intrinsic
qualities, the measure of life or power which it holds.
This ideal was neither the scholar nor the priest,
nor any type of the genteel or exceptionally favored
or cultivated. His influence does not make for any

form of depleted, indoor, over-refined or extra-cultured humanity. The spirit of his work trans-ferred to practice begets a life full and strong on all sides, affectionate, magnetic, tolerant, spiritual, bold with the flavor and quality of simple, healthful, open-air humanity. He opposes culture and refine-ment only as he opposes that which weakens, drains, emasculates, and tends to beget a scoffing, carping, hypercritical class. The culture of life, of nature, and that which flows from the exercise of the manly instincts and affections, is the culture implied by "Leaves of Grass." The democratic spirit is un-doubtedly more or less jealous of the refinements of our artificial culture and of the daintiness and aloofness of our literature. The people look askance at men who are above them without being of them, who have dropped the traits and attractions which they share with unlettered humanity. Frank-lin and Lincoln are closer akin to this spirit, and hence more in favor with it, than a Jefferson or a Sumner.

Whitman might be called the poet of the abso-lute, the unconditioned. His work is launched at a farther remove from our arts, conventions, usages, civilization, and all the artificial elements that mod-ify and enter into our lives, than that of any other man. Absolute candor, absolute pride, absolute charity, absolute social and sexual equality, absolute nature. It is not conditioned by what we deem modest or immodest, high or low, male or female. It is not conditioned by our notions of good and evil, by our notions of the refined and the select, by what we call good taste and bad taste. It is the voice of absolute man, sweeping away the artificial, throwing himself boldly, joyously, upon unconditional nature. We are all engaged in upholding the correct and the conventional, and drawing the line sharply between good and evil, the high and the low, and it is well that we should; but here is a man who aims to take absolute ground, and to look at the world as God himself might look at it, without partiality or discriminating, — it is all good, and there is no failure or imperfection in the universe and can be none: —

"Open mouth of my Soul uttering gladness,
   Eyes of my Soul seeing perfection,
   Natural life of me, faithfully praising things,
   Corroborating forever the triumph of things."

He does not take sides against evil, in the usual way, he does not take sides with the good except as nature herself does. He celebrates the All.

Can we accept the world as science reveals it to us, as all significant, as all in ceaseless transmutation, as every atom aspiring to be man, an endless unfolding of primal germs, without beginning, without end, without failure or imperfection, the golden age ahead of us, not behind us?

247

VIII

Because of Whitman's glorification of pride, egoism, brawn, self-reliance, it is charged that the noble, the cultured, the self-denying, have no place in his system. What place have they in the antique bards? — in Homer, in Job, in Isaiah, in Dante? They have the same place in Whitman, yet it is to be kept in mind that Whitman does not stand for the specially social virtues, nor for culture, nor for the refinements which it induces, nor for art, nor for any conventionality. There are flowers of human life which we are not to look for in Walt Whitman. The note of fine manners, chivalrous conduct, which we get in Emerson; the sweetness and light gospel of Arnold; the gospel of hero-worship of Carlyle; the gracious scholarship of our New England poets, etc., — we do not get in Walt Whitman. There is nothing in him at war with these things, but he is concerned with more primal and elemental questions. He strikes under and beyond all these things.

What are the questions or purposes, then, in which his work has root? Simply put, to lead the way to larger, saner, more normal, more robust types of men and women on this continent; to prefigure and help develop the new democratic man, — to project him into literature on a scale and with a distinctness that cannot be mistaken. To this

end he keeps a deep hold of the savage, the unrefined, and marshals the elements and influences that
make for the virile, the heroic, the sane, the large,
and for the perpetuity of the race. We cannot re-
fine the elements, — the air, the water, the soil, the
sunshine, — and the more we pervert or shut out
these from our lives the worse for us. In the same
manner, the more we pervert or balk the great
natural impulses, sexuality, comradeship, the religious emotion, nativity, or the more we deny and
belittle our bodies, the further we are from the
spirit of Walt Whitman, and from the spirit of the
All.

With all Whitman's glorification of pride, self-
esteem, self-reliance, etc., the final lesson of his life
and work is service, self-denial, — the free, lavish
giving of yourself to others. Of the innate and
essential nobility that we associate with unworld-
liness, the sharing of what you possess with the
unfortunate around you, sympathy with all forms of
life and conditions of men, charity as broad as the
sunlight, standing up for those whom others are
down upon, claiming nothing for self which others
may not have upon the same terms, — of such
nobility and fine manners, I say, you shall find an
abundance in the life and works of Walt Whitman.

The spirit of a man's work is everything; the
letter, little or nothing. Though Whitman boasts of
his affiliation with the common and near at hand,

yet he is always saved from the vulgar, the mean, the humdrum, by the breadth of his charity and sympathy and his tremendous ideality.

Of worldliness, materialism, commercialism, he has not a trace; his only values are spiritual and ideal; his only standards are the essential and the enduring. What Matthew Arnold called the Anglo-Saxon contagion, the bourgeois spirit, the worldly and sordid ideal, is entirely corrected in Whitman by the ascendant of the ethic and the universal. His democracy ends in universal brotherhood, his patriotism in the solidarity of nations, his glorification of the material in the final triumph of the spiritual, his egoism issues at last in complete altruism.

A race that can produce a man of his fibre, his continental type, is yet at its best estate. Did one begin to see evil omen in this perpetual whittling away and sharpening and lightening of the American type, — grace without power, clearness without mass, intellect without character? Then take comfort from the volume and the rankness of Walt Whitman. Did one begin to fear that the decay of maternity and paternity in our older communities and the falling off in the native population presaged the drying up of the race in its very sources? Then welcome to the rank sexuality and to the athletic fatherhood and motherhood celebrated by Whitman. Did our skepticism, our headiness, our worldliness, threaten to eat us up like a cancer? did our hardness, our irreligiousness, and our passion for the genteel point to a fugitive, superficial race? was our literature threatened with the artistic degeneration, — running all to art and not at all to power? were our communities invaded by a dry rot of culture? were we fast becoming a delicate, indoor, genteel race? were our women sinking deeper and deeper into the "incredible sloughs of fashion and all kinds of dyspeptic depletion," — the antidote for all these ills is in Walt Whitman. In him nature shows great fullness and fertility, and an immense friendliness. He supplements and corrects most of the special deficiencies and weaknesses toward which the American type seems to tend. He brings us back to nature again. The perpetuity of the race is with the common people. The race is constantly dying out at the top, in our times at least; culture and refinement beget fewer and fewer and poorer and poorer children. Where struggle ceases, that family or race is doomed.

"Now understand me well — it is provided in the essence of things that from any fruition of success, no matter what, shall come forth something to make a greater struggle necessary."

In more primitive communities, the sap and vitality of the race were kept in the best men, because upon them the strain and struggle were greatest.

War, adventure, discovery, favor virility. Whitman is always and everywhere occupied with that which makes for life, power, longevity, manliness. The scholar poets are occupied with that which makes for culture, taste, refinement, ease, art.

"Leaves of Grass," taken as a whole, aims to exhibit a modern, democratic, archetypal man, here in America, confronting and subduing our enormous materialism to his own purposes, putting it off and on as a garment; identifying himself with all forms of life and conditions of men; trying himself by cosmic laws and processes, exulting in the life of his body and the delights of his senses; and seeking to clinch, to develop, and to realize himself through the shows and events of the visible world. The poet seeks to interpret life from the central point of absolute abysmal man.

The wild and the savage in nature with which Whitman perpetually identifies himself, and the hirsute, sun-tanned, and aboriginal in humanity, have misled many readers into looking upon him as expressive of these things only. Mr. Stedman thinks him guilty of a certain narrowness in preferring, or seeming to prefer, the laboring man to the gentleman. But the poet uses these elements only for checks and balances, and to keep our attention, in the midst of a highly refined and civilized age, fixed upon the fact that here are the final sources of our health, our power, our longevity. The need

of the pre-scientific age was knowledge and refinement; the need of our age is health and sanity, cool
heads and good digestion. And to this end the bitter
and drastic remedies from the shore and the mountains are for us.

IX

The gospel of the average man, Matthew Arnold
thought, was inimical to the ideal of a rare and high
excellence. But, in holding up the average man,
Whitman was only holding up the broad, universal
human qualities, and showing that excellence may
go with them also. As a matter of fact, are we not
astonished almost daily by the superb qualities
shown by the average man, the heroism shown by
firemen, engineers, workingmen, soldiers, sailors?
Do we not know that true greatness, true nobility
and strength of soul, may go and do go with commonplace, every-day humanity? Whitman would
lift the average man to a higher average, and still
to a higher, without at all weakening the qualities
which he shares with universal humanity as it exists
over and under all special advantages and social
refinements. He says that one of the convictions
that underlie his "Leaves" is the conviction that
the "crowning growth of the United States is to be
spiritual and heroic," — a prophecy which in our
times, I confess, does not seem very near fulfillment.

He does not look longingly and anxiously toward the genteel social gods, but quite the contrary. In the library and parlor, he confesses he is as a gawk or one dumb. The great middle-class ideal, which is mainly the ideal of our own people, Whitman flouts and affronts. There are things to him of higher import than to have wealth and be respectable and in the mode.

We might charge him with narrowness and partiality and with seeing only half truths, as Mr. Stedman has done, did he simply rest with the native as opposed to the cultivated, with brawn as opposed to brains. What he does do, what the upshot of his teaching shows, is that he identifies himself with the masses, with those universal human currents out of which alone a national spirit arises, as opposed to isolated schools and coteries and a privileged few. Whitman decries culture only so far as it cuts off from his fellows, clips away or effaces the sweet, native, healthy parts of him, and begets a bloodless, superstitious, infidelistic class. "The best culture," he says, "will always be that of the manly and courageous instincts and loving perceptions, and of self-respect." For the most part, our schooling is like our milling, which takes the bone- and nerve-building elements out of our bread. The bread of life demands the coarse as well as the fine, and this is what Whitman stands for.

In his spirit and affiliation with the great mass

of the people, with the commoner, sturdier, human traits, Whitman is more of the type of Angelo, or Rembrandt, or the antique bards, than he is like modern singers. He was not a product of the schools, but of the race.

HIS RELATION TO HIS COUNTRY AND HIS TIMES

I

IT has been said, and justly I think, that in Whitman we see the first appearance in literature of the genuinely democratic spirit on anything like an ample scale. Plenty of men of democratic tendencies and affiliations have appeared, but none that have carried the temper and quality of the people, the masses, into the same regions, or blended the same humanity and commonness with the same commanding personality and spirituality. In recent English poetry the names of Burns and Wordsworth occur to mind, but neither of these men had anything like Whitman's breadth of relation to the mass of mankind, or expressed anything like his sweeping cosmic emotion. Wordsworth's muse was clad in homespun, but in no strict sense was his genius democratic — using the word to express, not a political creed, but the genius of modern civilization. He made much of the common man, common life, common things, but always does the poet stand apart, the recluse, the hermit, the philosopher, loving and contemplating these things for purposes of his art. Only through intellectual sympathy is he a part of what he surveys. In Whitman the common or average man has grown haughty, almost aristocratic. He coolly confronts the old types, the man of caste, culture, privileges, royalties, and relegates him to the past. He readjusts the standards, and estimates everything from the human and democratic point of view. In his scheme, the old traditions — the aristocratic, the scholastic, the ecclesiastical, the military, the social traditions — play no part. He dared to look at life, past and present, from the American and scientific standpoint. He turns to the old types a pride and complacency equal to their own.

Indeed, we see in the character which Whitman has exploited and in the interest of which his poems are written, the democratic type fully realized, — pride and self-reliance equal to the greatest, and these matched with a love, a compassion, a spirit of fraternity and equality, that are entirely foreign to the old order of things.

II

At first sight Whitman does not seem vitally related to his own country and people; he seems an anomaly, an exception, or like one of those mammoth sports that sometimes appear in the vegetable world. The Whitman ideal is not, and has never been, the conscious ideal of the mass of our people.

HIS RELATION TO HIS COUNTRY

We have aspired more to the ideal of the traditional fine gentleman as he has figured in British letters. There seems to have been no hint or prophecy of such a man as Whitman in our New England literature, unless it be in Emerson, and here it is in the region of the abstract and not of the concrete. Emerson's prayer was for the absolutely self-reliant man, but when Whitman refused to follow his advice with regard to certain passages in the "Leaves," the sage withheld further approval of the work.

We must look for the origins of Whitman, I think, in the deep world-currents that have been shaping the destinies of the race for the past hundred years or more; in the universal loosening, freeing, and removing obstructions; in the emancipation of the people, and their coming forward and taking possession of the world in their own right; in the triumph of democracy and of science; the downfall of kingcraft and priestcraft; the growth of individualism and non-conformity; the increasing disgust of the soul of man with forms and ceremonies; the sentiment of realism and positivism, the religious hunger that flees the churches; the growing conviction that life, that nature, are not failures, that the universe is good, that man is clean and divine inside and out, that God is immanent in nature, — all these things and more lie back of Whitman, and hold a causal relation to him.

III

Of course the essential elements of all first-class artistic and literary productions are always the same, just as nature, just as man, are essentially the same everywhere. Yet the literature of every people has a stamp of its own, starts from and implies antecedents and environments peculiar to itself.

Just as ripe, mellow, storied, ivy-towered, velvet-turfed England lies back of Tennyson, and is vocal through him; just as canny, covenanting, conscience-burdened, craggy, sharp-tongued Scotland lies back of Carlyle; just as thrifty, well-schooled, well-housed, prudent, and moral New England lies back of her group of poets, and is voiced by them, — so America as a whole, our turbulent democracy, our self-glorification, our faith in the future, our huge mass movements, our continental spirit, our sprawling, sublime, and unkempt nature, lie back of Whitman and are implied by his work.

He had not the shaping, manipulating gift to carve his American material into forms of ideal beauty, and did not claim to have. He did not value beauty as an abstraction.

What Whitman did that is unprecedented, was to take up the whole country into himself, fuse it, imbue it with soul and poetic emotion, and recast it as a sort of colossal Walt Whitman. He has not so much treated American themes as he has identified himself with everything American, and made the whole land redolent of his own quality. He has descended upon the gross materialism of our day and land and upon the turbulent democratic masses with such loving impact, such fervid enthusiasm, as to lift and fill them with something like the breath of universal nature. His special gift is his magnetic and unconquerable personality, his towering egoism united with such a fund of human sympathy. His power is centripetal, so to speak, — he draws everything into himself like a maelstrom; the centrifugal power of the great dramatic artists, the power to get out of and away from himself, he has not. It was not for Whitman to write the dramas and tragedies of democracy, as Shakespeare wrote those of feudalism, or as Tennyson sang in delectable verse the swan-song of an over-ripe civilization. It was for him to voice the democratic spirit, to show it full-grown, athletic, haughtily taking possession of the world and redistributing the prizes according to its own standards. It was for him to sow broadcast over the land the germs of larger, more sane, more robust types of men and women, indicating them in himself.

In him the new spirit of democracy first completely knows itself, is proud of itself, has faith and joy in itself, is fearless, tolerant, religious, aggressive, triumphant, and bestows itself lavishly upon all sides. It is tentative, doubtful, hesitating no longer. It is at ease in the world, it takes possession, it fears no rival, it advances with confident step.

No man was ever more truly fathered by what is formative and expansive in his country and times than was Whitman. Not by the literature of his country was he begotten, but by the spirit that lies back of all, and that begat America itself, — the America that Europe loves and fears, that she comes to this country to see, and looks expectantly, but for the most part vainly, in our books to find.

It seems to me he is distinctly a continental type. His sense of space, of magnitude, his processional pages, his unloosedness, his wide horizons, his vanishing boundaries, — always something unconfined and unconfinable, always the deferring and undemonstrable. The bad as well as the good traits of his country and his people are doubtless implied by his work.

If he does not finally escape from our unripe Americanism, if he does not rise through it all and clarify it and turn it to ideal uses, draw out the spiritual meanings, then avaunt! we want nothing of him.

"The pleasures of heaven are with me and the pains of
        hell.
The former I graft and increase upon myself,
The latter I translate into a new tongue."

HIS RELATION TO HIS COUNTRY

The vital and the formative the true poet always engrafts and increases upon himself, and thence upon his reader; the crude, the local, the accidental, he translates into a new tongue. It has been urged against Whitman that he expresses our unripe Americanism only, but serious readers of him know better than that. He is easy master of it all, and knows when his foot is upon solid ground. It seems to me that in him we see for the first time spiritual and ideal meanings and values in democracy and the modern; we see them translated into character; we see them tried by universal standards; we see them vivified by a powerful imagination. We see America as an idea, and see its relation to other ideas. We get a new conception of the value of the near, the common, the familiar. New light is thrown upon the worth and significance of the common people, and it is not the light of an abstract idea, but the light of a concrete example. We see the democratic type on a scale it has never before assumed; it is on a par with any of the types that have ruled the world in the past, the military, the aristocratic, the regal. It is at home, it has taken possession, it can hold its own. Henceforth the world is going its way. If it is over-confident, over-self-assertive, too American, that is the surplusage of the poet, of whom we do not want a penny prudence and caution; make your prophecy bold enough and it fulfills itself. Whitman has betrayed no doubt or hesitation in his poetry.

WHITMAN

His assumptions and vaticinations are tremendous, but they are uttered with an authority and an assurance that convince like natural law.

IV

I think he gives new meaning to democracy and America. In him we see a new type, rising out of new conditions, and fully able to justify itself and hold its own. It is the new man in the new world, no longer dependent upon or facing toward the old. I confess that to me America and the modern would not mean very much without Whitman. The final proof was wanting till they gave birth to a personality equal to the old types.

Discussions and speculations about democracy do not carry very far, after all; to preach equality is not much. But when we see these things made into a man, and see the world through his eyes, and see new joy and new meaning in it, our doubts and perplexities are cleared up. Our universal balloting, and schooling, and material prosperity prove nothing: can your democracy produce a man who shall carry its spirit into loftiest regions, and prove as helpful and masterful under the new conditions as the by-gone types were under the old?

HIS RELATION TO HIS COUNTRY

V

I predict a great future for Whitman, because the world is so unmistakably going his way. The three or four great currents of the century — the democratic current, the scientific current, the humanitarian current, the new religious current, and what flows out of them — are underneath all Whitman has written. They shape all and make all. They do not appear in him as mere dicta, or intellectual propositions, but as impulses, will, character, flesh-and-blood reality. We get these things, not as sentiments or yet theories, but as a man. We see life and the world as they appear to the inevitable democrat, the inevitable lover, the inevitable believer in God and immortality, the inevitable acceptor of absolute science.

We are all going his way. We are more and more impatient of formalities, ceremonies, and make-believe; we more and more crave the essential, the real. More and more we want to see the thing as in itself it is; more and more is science opening our eyes to see the divine, the illustrious, the universal in the common, the near at hand; more and more do we tire of words and crave things; deeper and deeper sinks the conviction that personal qualities alone tell, — that the man is all in all, that the brotherhood of the race is not a dream, that love covers all and atones for all.

WHITMAN

Everything in our modern life and culture that tends to broaden, liberalize, free; that tends to make hardy, self-reliant, virile; that tends to widen charity, deepen affection between man and man, to foster sanity and self-reliance; that tends to kindle our appreciation of the divinity of all things; that heightens our rational enjoyment of life; that inspires hope in the future and faith in the unseen, — are on Whitman's side. All these things prepare the way for him.

On the other hand, the strain and strife and hoggishness of our civilization, our trading politics, our worship of conventions, our millionaire ideals, our high-pressure lives, our pruriency, our sordidness, our perversions of nature, our scoffing caricaturing tendencies, are against him. He antagonizes all these things.

The more democratic we become, the more we are prepared for Whitman; the more tolerant, fraternal, sympathetic we become, the more we are ready for Whitman; the more we inure ourselves to the open air and to real things, the more we value and understand our own bodies, the more the woman becomes the mate and equal of the man, the more social equality prevails, — the sooner will come to Whitman fullness and fruition.

HIS RELATION TO HIS COUNTRY

VI

Some of our own critics have been a good deal annoyed by the fact that many European scholars and experts have recognized Whitman as the only distinctive American poet thus far. It would seem as if our reputation for culture and good manners is at stake. We want Europe to see America in our literary poets like Lowell, or Longfellow, or Whittier. And Europe may well see much that is truly representative of America in these and in other New England poets. She may see our aspiration toward her own ideals of culture and refinement; she may see native and patriotic themes firing Lowell and Whittier; she may see a certain spirit and temper begotten by our natural environment reflected in Bryant, our delicate and gentle humanities and scholarly aptitudes shining in Longfellow. But in every case she sees a type she has long been familiar with. All the poets' thoughts, moods, points of view, effects, aims, methods, are what she has long known. These are not the poets of a new *world*, but of a new *England*. The new-world book implies more than a new talent, more than a fresh pair of eyes, a fresh and original mind like the poets named; such men are required to keep up the old line of succession in English authorship. What is implied is a new national and continental spirit, which must arise and voice the old eternal truths

267

through a large, new, democratic personality, — **a** new man, and, beyond and above him, a new heaven and a new earth.

Our band of New England poets have carried the New England spirit into poetry, — its sense of fitness, order, propriety, its shrewdness, inventiveness, aptness, and its aspiration for the pure and noble in life. They have finely exemplified the best Yankee traits; but in no instance were these traits merged in a personality large enough, bold enough, and copious and democratic enough to give them national and continental significance. It would be absurd to claim that the pulse-beat of a great people or a great era is to be felt in the work of any of these poets.

Whitman is responded to in Europe, because he expresses a new type with adequate power, — not, as has been so often urged, simply because he is strange, and gives the jaded literary palate over there a new fillip. He meets the demand for something in American literature that should not face toward Europe, that should joyfully stand upon its own ground and yet fulfill the conditions of greatness. He fully satisfies the thirst for individualism amid these awakening peoples, and the thirst for nationalism also. He realizes the democratic ideal, no longer tentative or apologetic, but taking possession of the world as its own and reappraising the wares it finds there.

VII

The American spirit is a continental spirit; there is nothing insular or narrow about it. It is informal, nonchalant, tolerant, sanguine, adaptive, patient, candid, puts up with things, unfastidious, unmindful of particulars; disposed to take short cuts, friendly, hospitable, unostentatious, inclined to exaggerate, generous, unrefined, — never meddlesome, never hypercritical, never hoggish, never exclusive. Whitman shared the hopeful optimistic temperament of his countrymen, the faith and confidence begotten by a great, fertile, sunny land. He expresses the independence of the people, — their pride, their jealousy of superiors, their contempt of authority (not always beautiful). Our want of reverence and veneration are supplemented in him with world-wide sympathies and good-fellowship.

Emerson is our divine man, the precious quintessence of the New England type, invaluable for his stimulating and ennobling strain; but his genius is too astral, too select, too remote, to incarnate and give voice to the national spirit. Clothe him with flesh and blood, make his daring affirmations real and vital in a human personality and imbued with the American spirit, and we are on the way to Whitman.

Moreover, the strong, undisguised man-flavor of "Leaves of Grass," the throb and pressure in it of

269

those things that make life rank and make it masterful, and that make for the virility and perpetuity of the race, are, if it must be confessed, more keenly relished abroad than in this country, so thoroughly are we yet under the spell of the merely refined and conventional. We fail to see that in letters, as in life, the great prizes are not to the polished, but to the virile and the strong.

VIII

Democracy is not so much spoken of in the "Leaves" as it is it that speaks. The common, the familiar, are not denied and left behind, they are made vital and masterful ; it is the "divine average" that awakens enthusiasm. Humanity is avenged upon the scholar and the "gentleman" for the slights they have put upon it; creeds and schools in abeyance; personal qualities, force of character, to the front. Whitman triumphs over the mean, the vulgar, the commonplace, by accepting them and imbuing them with the spirit of an heroic ideal. Wherever he reveals himself in his work, it is as one of the common people, never as one of a coterie or of the privileged and cultivated. He is determined there shall be no mistake about it. He glories in the common heritage. He emphasizes in himself the traits which he shares with workingmen, sailors, soldiers, and those who live in the open air, even laying claim to the "rowdyish." He is proud of freckles, sun-tan, brawn, and holds up the powerful and unrefined.

"I am enamour'd of growing out-doors,
Of men that live among cattle or taste of the ocean or woods,
Of the builders and steerers of ships and the wielders of axes and mauls, and the drivers of horses;
I can eat and sleep with them week in and week out."

"Nothing endures," he says, "but personal qualities." "Produce great persons and the rest follows." Does he glory in the present? he reverently bows before the past also. Does he sound the call of battle for the Union? but he nourishes the sick and wounded of the enemy as well. Does he flout at the old religions? but he offers a larger religion in their stead. He is never merely negative, he is never fanatical, he is never narrow. He sees all and embraces and encloses all.

Then we see united and harmonized in Whitman the two great paramount tendencies of our time and of the modern world, — the altruistic or humanitarian tendency and the individualistic tendency; or, democracy and individualism, pride and equality, or, rather, pride in equality. These two forces, as they appear in separate individuals, are often antagonistic. In Carlyle, individualism frowned upon democracy. In Whitman they are blended and work together. Never was such audacious and

271

uncompromising individualism, and never was such bold and sweeping fraternalism or altruism. The great pride of man in himself, which is one motif of the poems, flows naturally into the great pride of man in his fellows; his egoism does not separate him from, but rather unites him with, all men. What he assumes they shall assume, and what he claims for himself he demands in the same terms for all. He has set such an example of self-trust and self-assertion as has no parallel in our literature, at the same time that he has set an equal example in practical democracy and universal brotherhood.

IX

Whitman's democracy is the breath of his nostrils, the light of his eyes, the blood in his veins. The reader does not feel that here is some fine scholar, some fine poet singing the praises of democracy; he feels that here is a democrat, probably, as Thoreau surmised, the greatest the world has yet seen, turning the light of a great love, a great intellect, a great soul, upon America, upon contemporary life and events, and upon the universe, and reading new lessons, new meanings, therein. He is a great poet and prophet, speaking through the average man, speaking as one of the people, and interpreting life from the point of view of absolute democracy.

True, the people in their average taste and perceptions are crude and flippant and superficial, and
often the victims of mountebanks and fools; yet,
as forming the body of our social and political
organism, and the chief factor in the world-problem
of to-day, they are the exponents of great forces
and laws, and often, in emergencies, show the wisdom and unimpeachableness of Nature herself.
Deep-hidden currents and forces in them are liable
to come to the surface, and when the politicians
get in their way, or miscalculate them, as so often
happens, they are crushed. Whitman is a projection into literature of the cosmic sense and conscience of the people, and their participation in the
forces that are shaping the world in our century.
Much comes to a head in him, much comes to joyous speech and song, that heretofore had only come
to thought and speculation. A towering, audacious
personality has appeared which is strictly the fruit
of the democratic spirit, and which has voiced itself
in an impassioned utterance touching the whole
problem of national and individual life.

x

The Whitman literature is democratic, not in the
sense that it caters to the taste of the masses or to
the taste of the average man; for, as a matter of
fact, the masses and the average man are likely to
be the last to recognize its value. The common

people, the average newspaper-reading citizens, are much more likely to be drawn by the artificial and the conventional. But it is democratic because it is filled with the spirit of absolute human equality and brotherhood, and gives out the atmosphere of the universal, primary, human traits. The social, artificial, accidental distinctions of wealth, culture, position, etc., have not influenced the poet in the slightest degree. Whitman finds his joy and his triumph, not in being better than other people or above them, but in being one with them, and sharing their sins as well as their virtues.

> "As if it harm'd me, giving others the same chances and
> rights as myself — as if it were not indispensable
> to my own rights that others possess the same."

This is one step further than others have taken, and makes democracy complete in itself. Again, his work identifies itself with the democratic ideal in getting rid of the professional and arbitrary elements of poetry, and appealing to the reader entirely through its spirit and content. It is as democratic in this respect as the workman in the field, or the mechanic at his bench.

The poems are bathed and flooded with the quality of the common people; with the commonness and nearness which they share with real things and with all open-air nature, — with hunters, travelers, soldiers, workers in all fields, and with rocks, trees, better than he that in the long run the conditions of life and of human happiness and progress remain about the same; that the same price must still be paid for the same things; that character alone counts; that the same problem "how to live" ever confronts us; and that democracy, America, nationality, are only way-stations, and by no means the end of the route. The all-leveling tendency of democracy is certainly not in the interest of literature. The world is not saved by the average man, but by the man much above the average, the rare and extraordinary man, — by the "remnant," as Arnold called them.

No one knew this better than Whitman, and he said that "one main genesis-motive" of his "Leaves" was the conviction that the crowning growth of the United States was to be spiritual and heroic. Only "superb persons" can finally justify him.

HIS RELATION TO SCIENCE

I

THE stupendous disclosures of modern science, and what they mean when translated into the language of man's ethical and æsthetic nature, have not yet furnished to any considerable extent the inspiration of poems. That all things are alike divine, that this earth is a star in the heavens, that the celestial laws and processes are here underfoot, that size is only relative, that good and bad are only relative, that forces are convertible and interchangeable, that matter is indestructible, that death is the law of life, that man is of animal origin, that the sum of forces is constant, that the universe is a complexus of powers inconceivably subtle and vital, that motion is the law of all things, — in fact, that we have got rid of the notions of the absolute, the fixed, the arbitrary, and the notion of origins and of the dualism of the world, — to what extent will these and kindred ideas modify art and all æsthetic production? The idea of the divine right of kings and the divine authority of priests is gone; that in some other time or some other place God was nearer man than now and here, — this idea is gone. Indeed, the whole of man's spiritual and religious belief which forms the background of literature has

changed, — a change as great as if the sky were to
change from blue to red or to orange. The light
of day is different. But literature deals with life,
and the essential conditions of life, you say, always
remain the same. Yes, but the expression of their
artistic values is forever changing. If we ask where
is the modern imaginative work that is based upon
these revelations of science, the work in which they
are the blood and vital juices, I answer, "Leaves of
Grass," and no other. The work is the outgrowth
of science and modern ideas, just as truly as Dante
is the outgrowth of mediæval ideas and superstitions;
and the imagination, the creative spirit, is just as
unhampered in Whitman as in Dante or in Shakespeare. The poet finds the universe just as plastic
and ductile, just as obedient to his will, and just as
ready to take the impress of his spirit, as did these
supreme artists. Science has not hardened it at all.
The poet opposes himself to it, and masters it and
rises superior. He is not balked or oppressed for a
moment. He knows from the start what science can
bring him, what it can give, and what it can take
away; he knows the universe is not orphaned; he
finds more grounds than ever for a pæan of thanks-
giving and praise. His conviction of the identity of
soul and body, matter and spirit, does not shake his
faith in immortality in the least. His faith arises, not
from half views, but from whole views. In him the
idea of the soul, of humanity, of identity, easily

balanced the idea of the material universe. Man was more than a match for nature. It was all for him, and not for itself. His enormous egotism, or hold upon the central thought or instinct of human worth and import, was an anchor that never gave way. Science sees man as the ephemeron of an hour, an iridescent bubble on a seething, whirling torrent, an accident in a world of incalculable and clashing forces. Whitman sees him as inevitable and as immortal as God himself. Indeed, he is quite as egotistical and anthropomorphic, though in an entirely different way, as were the old bards and prophets before the advent of science. The whole import of the universe is directed to one man, — to you. His anthropomorphism is not a projection of himself into nature, but an absorption of nature in himself. The tables are turned. It is not alien or superhuman beings that he sees and hears in nature, but his own that he finds everywhere. All gods are merged in himself.

Not the least fear, not the least doubt or dismay, in this book. Not one moment's hesitation or losing of the way. And it is not merely an intellectual triumph, but the triumph of soul and personality. The iron knots are not untied, they are melted. Indeed, the poet's contentment and triumph in view of the fullest recognition of all the sin and sorrow of the world, and of all that baffles and dwarfs, is not the least of the remarkable features of the book.

II

Whitman's relation to science is fundamental and vital. It is the soil under his feet. He comes into a world from which all childish fear and illusion has been expelled. He exhibits the religious and poetic faculties perfectly adjusted to a scientific, industrial, democratic age, and exhibits them more fervent and buoyant than ever before. We have gained more than we have lost. The world is anew created by science and democracy, and he pronounces it good with the joy and fervor of the old faith.

He shared with Tennyson the glory of being one of the two poets of note in our time who have drawn inspiration from this source, or viewed the universe through the vistas which science opens. Renan thought the modern poetic or imaginative contemplation of the universe puerile and factitious compared with the scientific contemplation of it. The one, he said, was stupendous; the other childish and empty. But Whitman and Tennyson were fully abreast with science, and often afford one a sweep of vision that matches the best science can do. Tennyson drew upon science more for his images and illustrations than Whitman did; he did not absorb and appropriate its results in the wholesale way of the latter. Science fed Whitman's imagination and made him bold; its effects were moral and spiritual. On Tennyson its effects were mainly intellectual; it enlarged his vocabulary without strengthening his faith. Indeed, one would say, from certain passages in "In Memoriam," that it had distinctly weakened his faith. Let us note for a moment the different ways these two poets use science. In his poem to FitzGerald, Tennyson draws upon the nebular hypothesis for an image:

> "A planet equal to the sun
>> Which cast it, that large infidel
>> Your Omar."

In "Despair" there crops out another bold inference of science, the vision "of an earth that is dead."

> "The homeless planet at length will be wheel'd thro' the
>> silence of space,
> Motherless evermore of an ever-vanishing race."

In the "Epilogue" he glances into the sidereal heavens: —

> "The fires that arch this dusky dot —
>> Yon myriad-worlded way —
> The vast sun-clusters' gather'd blaze,
>> World-isles in lonely skies,
> Whole heavens within themselves, amaze
>> Our brief humanities."

As our American poet never elaborates in the Tennysonian fashion, he does not use science as material, but as inspiration. His egoism and an-

thropomorphic tendency are as great as those of the
early bards, and he makes everything tell for
the individual. Let me give a page or two from the
"Song of Myself," illustrative of his attitude in
this respect: —

> "I find I incorporate gneiss, coal, long-threaded moss,
> fruits, grains, esculent roots,
> And am stuccoed with quadrupeds and birds all over,
> And have distanced what is behind me for good reasons,
> And call anything close again, when I desire it.

> "In vain the speeding or shyness,
> In vain the plutonic rocks send their old heat against any
> approach,
> In vain the mastodon retreats beneath its own powdered
> bones,
> In vain objects stand leagues off, and assume manifold
> shapes,
> In vain the ocean settling in hollows, and the great
> monsters lying low,
> In vain the buzzard houses herself with the sky,
> In vain the snake slides through the creepers and logs,
> In vain the elk takes to the inner passes of the woods,
> In vain the razor-billed auk sails far north to Labrador,
> I follow quickly, I ascend to the nest in the fissure of the
> cliff.

. . . .

> "I am an acme of things accomplished, and I am an
> endorser of things to be.
> My feet strike an apex of the apices of the stairs,

HIS RELATION TO SCIENCE

On every step bunches of ages, and large bunches between
    the steps,
All below duly traveled, and still I mount and mount.

  "Rise after rise bow the phantoms behind me,
Afar down I see the huge first Nothing — I know I was
    even there,
I waited unseen and always, and slept through the
    lethargic mist,
And took my time, and took no hurt from the fetid carbon.

  "Long I was hugged close — long and long.
Immense have been the preparations for me,
Faithful and friendly the arms that have helped me,
Cycles ferried my cradle, rowing and rowing like cheer-
    ful boatmen,
For room to me stars kept aside in their own rings,
They sent influences to look after what was to hold me.

  "Before I was born out of my mother, generations
    guided me,
My embryo has never been torpid — nothing could
    overlay it.
For it the nebula cohered to an orb,
The long, slow strata piled to rest it in,
Vast vegetables gave it sustenance,
Monstrous sauroids transported it in their mouths, and
    deposited it with care.
All forces have been steadily employed to complete and
    delight me,
Now I stand on this spot with my Soul.

WHITMAN

"I open my scuttle at night and see the far-sprinkled
systems,
And all I see, multiplied as high as I can cipher, edge but
the rim of the farther systems:
Wider and wider they spread, expanding, always ex-
panding,
Outward, outward, and forever outward:
My sun has his sun, and around him obediently wheels;
He joins with his partners a group of superior circuit,
And greater sets follow, making specks of the greatest
inside them.

"There is no stoppage, and never can be stoppage;
If I, you, the worlds, all beneath or upon their surfaces,
and all the palpable life, were this moment reduced
back to a pallid float, it would not avail in the long
run.
We should surely bring up again where we now stand,
And as surely go as much farther — and then farther and
farther.
A few quadrillions of eras, a few octillions of cubic
leagues, do not hazard the span to make it impa-
tient.
They are but parts — anything is but a part,
See ever so far, there is limitless space outside of that,
Count ever so much, there is limitless time around that."

In all cases, Whitman's vision is as large as that of
science, but it is always the vision of a man and
not that of a philosopher. His report of the facts
has an imaginative lift and a spiritual significance

which the man of science cannot give them. In him, for the first time, a personality has appeared that cannot be dwarfed and set aside by those things. He does not have to stretch himself at all to match in the human and emotional realm the stupendous discoveries and deductions of science. In him man refuses to stand aside and acknowledge himself of no account in the presence of the cosmic laws and areas. It is all for him, it is all directed to him; without him the universe is an empty void. This is the "full-spread pride of man," the pride that refuses to own any master outside of itself.

"I know my omnivorous words, and cannot say any less,
And would fetch you, whoever you are, flush with myself."

HIS RELATION TO RELIGION

WHITMAN, as I have elsewhere said, was swayed by two or three great passions, and the chief of these was doubtless his religious passion. He thrilled to the thought of the mystery and destiny of the soul.

"The soul,
  Forever and forever — longer than soil is brown and
    solid — longer than water ebbs and flows."

He urged that there could be no permanent national grandeur, and no worthy manly or womanly development, without religion.

"I specifically announce that the real and permanent
    grandeur of these States must be their Religion,
  Otherwise there is no real and permanent grandeur."

All materials point to and end at last in spiritual results.

"Each is not for its own sake,
  I say the whole earth and all the stars in the sky are
    for Religion's sake."

All our ostensible realities, our art, our literature, our business pursuits, etc., are but fuel to religion.

"For not all matter is fuel to heat, impalpable flame, the
    essential life of the earth,
  Any more than such are to Religion."

Again he says: —

"My comrade!
  For you to share with me two greatnesses — And a
      third one, rising inclusive and more resplendent,
  The greatness of Love and Democracy — and the
      greatness of Religion."

It is hardly necessary to say that the religion
which Whitman celebrates is not any form of ecclesiasticism. It is larger than any creed that has
yet been formulated. It is the conviction of the
man of science touched and vivified by the emotion
of the prophet and poet. As exemplified in his
life its chief elements are faith, hope, charity.
Its object is to prepare you to live, not to die,
and to "earn for the body and the mind what
adheres and goes forward, and is not dropped by
death."

The old religion, the religion of our fathers, was
founded upon a curse. Sin, repentance, fear, Satan,
hell, play important parts. Creation had resulted
in a tragedy in which the very elemental forces
were implicated. The grand scheme of an infinite
Being failed through the machinations of the Devil.
Salvation was an escape from a wrath to come. The
way was through agony and tears. Heaven was only
gained by denying earth. The great mass of the
human race was doomed to endless perdition. Now
there is no trace of this religion in Whitman, and it

does not seem to have left any shadow upon him. Ecclesiasticism is dead; he clears the ground for a new growth. To the priests he says: "Your day is done."

He sings a new song; he tastes a new joy in life. The earth is as divine as heaven, and there is no god more sacred than yourself. It is as if the world had been anew created, and Adam had once more been placed in the garden, — the world, with all consequences of the fall, purged from him.

Hence we have in Whitman the whole human attitude toward the universe, toward God, toward life and death, toward good and evil, completely changed. We have absolute faith and acceptance in place of the fear and repentance of the old creeds; we have death welcomed as joyously as life, we have political and social equality as motifs and impulses, and not merely as sentiments. He would show us the muse of poetry, as impartial, as sweeping in its vision, as modern, as real, as free from the morbid and make-believe, as the muse of science. He sees good in all, beauty in all. It is not the old piety, it is the new faith; it is not the old worship, it is the new acceptance; not the old, corroding religious pessimism, but the new scientific optimism.

He does not deny, he affirms; he does not criticise, he celebrates; his is not a call to repentance, it is a call to triumph: —

WHITMAN

"I say no man has ever yet been half devout enough,
 None has ever yet adored or worship'd half enough,
 None has begun to think how divine he himself is, or
    how certain the future is."

He accepted science absolutely, yet science was not
an end in itself: it was not his dwelling; he but
entered by it to an area of his dwelling.

The flower of science was religion. Without this
religion, or something akin to it, — without some
spiritual, emotional life that centred about an ideal,
— Whitman urged that there could be no permanent
national or individual development. In the past
this ideal was found in the supernatural; for us and
the future democratic ages, it must be found in the
natural, in the now and the here.

The aristocratic tradition not only largely shaped
the literature of the past, it shaped the religion:
man was a culprit, his life a rebellion; his proper
attitude toward the unseen powers was that of a
subject to his offended sovereign, — one of prostra-
tion and supplication. Heaven was a select circle
reserved for the few, — the aristocracy of the pure
and just. The religion of a democratic and scientific era, as voiced by Whitman and as exemplified
in his life, is of quite another character, — not veneration, but joy and triumph; not fear, but love;
not self-abasement, but self-exaltation; not sacrifice, but service: in fact, not religion at all in the
old sense of the spiritual at war with the natural,

292

the divine with the human, this world a vale of tears, and mundane things but filth and ashes, heaven for the good and hell for the bad; but in the new sense of the divinity of all things, of the equality of gods and men, of the brotherhood of the race, of the identity of the material and the spiritual, of the beneficence of death and the perfection of the universe. The poet turns his face to earth and not to heaven; he finds the miraculous, the spiritual, in the things about him, and gods and goddesses in the men and women he meets. He effaces the old distinctions; he establishes a sort of universal suffrage in spiritual matters; there are no select circles, no privileged persons. Is this the democracy of religion? liberty, fraternity, and equality carried out in the spiritual sphere? Death is the right hand of God, and evil plays a necessary part also. Nothing is discriminated against; there are no reprisals or postponements, no dualism or devilism. Everything is in its place; man's life and all the things of his life are well considered.

Carried out in practice, this democratic religion will not beget priests, or churches, or creeds, or rituals, but a life cheerful and full on all sides, helpful, loving, unworldly, tolerant, open-souled, temperate, fearless, free, and contemplating with pleasure, rather than alarm, "the exquisite transition of death."

A FINAL WORD

AFTER all I have written about Whitman, I feel at times that the main thing I wanted to say about him I have not said, cannot say; the best about him cannot be told anyway. "My final merit I refuse you." His full significance in connection with the great modern movement; how he embodies it all and speaks out of it, and yet maintains his hold upon the primitive, the aboriginal; how he presupposes science and culture, yet draws his strength from that which antedates these things; how he glories in the present, and yet is sustained and justified by the past; how he is the poet of America and the modern, and yet translates these things into universal truths; how he is the poet of wickedness, while yet every fibre of him is sound and good; how his page is burdened with the material, the real, the contemporary, while yet his hold upon the ideal, the spiritual, never relaxes; how he is the poet of the body, while yet he is in even fuller measure the poet of the soul; in fact, how all contradictions are finally reconciled in him, — all these things and more, I say, I feel that I have not set forth with the clearness and emphasis the subject demanded. Other students of him will approach him on other lines, and will disclose meanings that I have missed.

Writing about him, as Symonds said, is enormously difficult. At times I feel as if I was almost as much at sea with regard to him as when I first began to study him; not at sea with regard to his commanding genius and power, but with regard to any adequate statement and summary of him in current critical terms. One cannot define and classify him as he can a more highly specialized poetic genius. What is he like? He is like everything. He is like the soil which holds the germs of a thousand forms of life; he is like the grass, common, universal, perennial, formless; he is like your own heart, mystical yearning, rebellious, contradictory, but ever throbbing with life. He is fluid, generative, electric; he is full of the germs, potencies, and latencies of things; he provokes thought without satisfying it; he is formless without being void; he is both Darwinian and Dantesque. He is the great reconciler, he united and harmonized so many opposites in himself. As a man he united the masculine and feminine elements in a remarkable degree; he united the innocent vanity of the child with the self-reliance of a god. In his moral aspects, he united egoism and altruism, pride and charity, individualism and democracy, fierce patriotism and the cosmopolitan spirit; in his literary aspects he united mysticism and realism, the poet

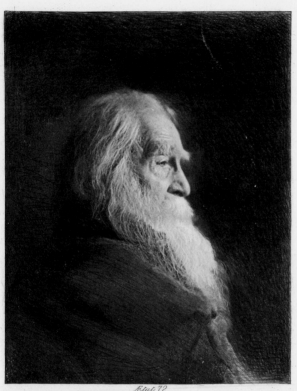

Ætat 72.

Walt Whitman

and prophet, the local and the universal; in his religious aspects he united faith and agnosticism, the glorification of the body and all objective things, with an unshakable trust in the reality of the invisible world.

Rich in the elements of poetry, a London critic says, almost beyond any other poet of his time, and yet carefully stopping short of the conscious, elaborate, crystallic, poetic work which the critic demanded of him, quite content to hold it all in solution, and give his reader an impulse rather than a specimen.

I have accepted Whitman entire and without reservation. I could not do otherwise. It was clear enough to me that he was to be taken as a whole or not at all. We cannot cut and carve a man. The latest poet brings us poetic wares, curiously and beautifully carved and wrought specimens, some of which we accept and some of which we pass by. Whitman brings us no cunning handicraft of the muses: he brings us a gospel, he brings us a man, he brings us a new revelation of life; and either his work appeals to us as a whole, or it does not so appeal. He will not live in separate passages, or in a few brief poems, any more than Shakespeare or Homer or Dante, or the Bible, so lives.

The chief thing about the average literary poet is his poetic gift, apart from any other consideration;

we select from what he brings us as we select from a basket of fruit. The chief thing about Whitman is the personality which the poetic gift is engaged in exploiting; the excitement of our literary or artistic sense is always less than the excitement of our sense of life and of real things. We get in him a fixed point of view, a new vantage-ground of personality from which to survey life. It is less what he brings, and more what he is, than with other poets. To take him by fragments, picking out poetic tidbits here and there, rejecting all the rest, were like valuing a walk through the fields and woods only for the flowers culled here and there, or the bits of color in the grass or foliage. Is the air, the sunshine, the free spaces, the rocks, the soil, the trees, and the exhilaration of it all, nothing? There are flowers in Whitman, too, but they are amid the rocks or under the trees, and seem quite unpremeditated and by the way, and never the main concern. If our quest is for these alone, we shall surely be disappointed. "In order to appreciate Whitman's poetry and his purpose," says Joel Chandler Harris, "it is necessary to possess the intuition that enables the mind to grasp in instant and express admiration the vast group of facts that make man, — that make liberty, — that make America. There is no poetry in the details; it is all in the broad, sweeping, comprehensive assimilation of the mighty forces behind them, — the inevitable, unaccountable, irresistible forward movement of man in the making of this Republic."

And again: "Those who approach Walt Whitman's poetry from the literary side are sure to be disappointed. Whatever else it is, it is not literary. Its art is its own, and the melody of it must be sought in other suggestions than those of metre. . . . Those who are merely literary will find little substance in the great drama of Democracy which is outlined by Walt Whitman in his writings, — it is no distinction to call them poems. But those who know nature at first hand — who know man, who see in this Republic something more than a political government — will find therein the thrill and glow of poetry and the essence of melody. Not the poetry that culture stands in expectation of, nor the melody that capers in verse and metre, but those rarer intimations and suggestions that are born in primeval solitudes, or come whirling from the vast funnel of the storm." How admirable! how true! No man has ever spoken more to the point upon Walt Whitman.

The appearance of such a man as Whitman involves deep world-forces of race and time. He is rooted in the very basic structure of his age. After what I have already said, my reader will not be surprised when I tell him that I look upon Whitman as the one mountain thus far in our literary landscape. To me he changes the whole aspect, almost the very climate, of our literature. He adds the much-needed ruggedness, breadth, audacity, independence, and the elements of primal strength and health. We owe much to Emerson. But Emerson was much more a *made* man than was Whitman, — much more the result of secondary forces, the college, the church, and of New England social and literary culture. With all his fervid humanity and deeply ingrained modernness, Whitman has the virtues of the primal and the savage. "Leaves of Grass" has not the charm, or the kind of charm, of the more highly wrought artistic works, but it has the incentive of nature and the charm of real things. We shall not go to it to be soothed and lulled. It will always remain among the difficult and heroic undertakings, demanding our best moments, our best strength, our morning push and power. Like voyaging or mountain-climbing, or facing any danger or hardship by land or sea, it fosters manly endeavor and the great virtues of sanity and self-reliance.

𝕮𝖍𝖊 𝕽𝖎𝖛𝖊𝖗𝖘𝖎𝖉𝖊 𝕻𝖗𝖊𝖘𝖘

Electrotyped and printed by H. O. Houghton & Co.
Camoridge, Mass, U. S. A.